THE JOURNALS OF
CHARLES W. CHESNUTT

The Journals of
Charles W. Chesnutt

RICHARD H. BRODHEAD,
EDITOR

Chesnutt, Charles Waddell.

DUKE UNIVERSITY PRESS   *Durham and London 1993*

Frontispiece: Charles Chesnutt in 1874, aged 16
© 1993 Duke University Press
All rights reserved
Printed in the United States of America on acid-free paper ∞
Typeset in New Baskerville by Tseng Information Systems
Library of Congress Cataloging-in-Publication Data
appear on the last printed page of this book.

CONTENTS

LIST OF ILLUSTRATIONS
VII

ACKNOWLEDGMENTS
IX

INTRODUCTION
I

A NOTE ON THE TEXT
37

FIRST JOURNAL, 1874–1875
39

SECOND JOURNAL, 1877–1881
85

THIRD JOURNAL, 1881–1882
157

INDEX
183

ILLUSTRATIONS

Charles W. Chesnutt in 1874, aged 16   frontispiece

Robert Harris, Chesnutt's Fayetteville teacher and superior at
the State Colored Normal School   29

Bishop Cicero Harris, Chesnutt's superior at the Peabody
School in Charlotte   30

The Howard School (later the State Colored Normal School),
Fayetteville, North Carolina   31

Charles W. Chesnutt around 1879, aged 21   32

The Perry Homestead, Fayetteville, Chesnutt's wife's family's
home, where he lived from 1878 to 1880   33

Character reference given to Chesnutt by Dr. T. D. Haigh,
chairman of the Board of Managers of the State Colored
Normal School, upon Chesnutt's departure from
Fayetteville in 1883   34

Charles Chesnutt in 1899 (the year of *The Conjure Woman*),
aged 41   35

ACKNOWLEDGMENTS

It is a pleasure to acknowledge the many forms of help I received in preparing this journal for publication. The keepers of the Special Collections at the Fisk University Library in Nashville, Beth Howse and Ann Shockley, gave me gracious assistance in my work with the Charles Waddell Chesnutt Papers. Kevis Goodman gave expert aid in transcribing parts of the second and third journals. Jeffrey and Christa Sammons deciphered Chesnutt's old-style German script with cheerful efficiency. LaJean P. Carruth brought her skills to bear on journal passages kept in Pittman shorthand. Mindy Conner copy edited the volume with exemplary care.

Daisy Maxwell's extraordinary command of local archival materials made it possible to identify many otherwise inscrutable figures and episodes from Chesnutt's Fayetteville years. The annotation of this volume would have been radically incomplete without her assistance. Walter J. Meserve and Charles H. Shattuck kindly answered inquiries about arcana of theater history. In addition to other help, Joel Williamson supplied the lead that made it possible to identify the historical referents of Chesnutt's poem "The Perplexed Nigger," about which Susan P. Walker of the United States Military Academy Archives provided further information. Valerie Burnie, of the Public Library of Charlotte and Mecklenburg County, helped identify several obscure references from Chesnutt's Charlotte journal. I had assistance as well from reference librarians at Davidson College, Fayetteville State University, Howard University, Yale University, the

Cumberland County (N.C.) Public Library, and the Spartanburg County (S.C.) Public Library. Joshua Rowland helped with the final stages of manuscript preparation. Cecilia Tichi provided good company during my Nashville stays.

All the illustrations are reproduced with the permission of the Fisk University Library Special Collections except the portrait of Robert Harris, which was provided with the assistance of the Fayetteville State University Library. Permission to reprint the journal has been given by Chesnutt's descendant John C. Slade.

THE JOURNALS OF
CHARLES W. CHESNUTT

INTRODUCTION

The Fisk University Library's Special Collections house a three-volume journal kept on and off for nine years in the late nineteenth century in a clear, confident hand. This journal has the paradoxical status that all such writing has. The record of the living, present moment of a fellow human's self-awareness, its aging paper reminds us that all such moments pass and die. But if it evokes the law of mortality, this writing also evades it, stretching forward to preserve a trace of the past for our present understanding. The journal's relation to the law of privacy is similarly two-sided. It is not written for us. The notion that strangers might someday read its pages exists only in the vainest of the author's fantasies. Yet as soon as we start to read it, this writing not addressed to us speaks to us, opens its writer's private thoughts to our public inspection.

This document shares the general fascination of papers exhumed from old trunks and boxes and drawers, in Faulkner's memorable phrase. But it also has more particular interests to justify its publication. First and most obviously, this journal was kept by an author who has been recognized as a major figure in African-American writing in the late nineteenth and early twentieth centuries, and who begins to be recognized as a major contributor to American literature at large. The stories of *The Conjure Woman* and *The Wife of His Youth* and the novels *The House Behind the Cedars* and *The Marrow of Tradition* are still far in the future when this journal ends, but these pages give an unusually detailed glimpse of the early life of the writer who went on to create those important works. Kept between 1874 and 1882, between his sixteenth and twenty-fourth years, these journals supply virtually all the evidence we have of Charles W. Chesnutt's evolving ambitions and of the world in which he framed those ambitions in his formative years.

Its authorship gives the journal part of its importance, then. But this work would be almost as resonant if its author were not known to us for other accomplishments. Quite apart from their relevance to the Chesnutt literary canon, these pages offer one of the great inside narratives of a classic American character type from the heyday of American individualism. The Journal of a Self-Made Man, as it might be titled—or the Journal of a Home Improver (a person who improves himself on his own), in Chesnutt's own phrase—Chesnutt's diary affords almost unmatched access to the inner workings of a real, historical self organized on a widely disseminated American cultural plan: the compulsive achiever, the self self-driven and self-disciplined toward future attainment, of which Ben Franklin is the national archetype.

The lack of external advantages forms a necessary part of the career history of this familiar character, and Chesnutt is no exception in this regard. But if Chesnutt presents a fairly standard exhibit of this type's inner disciplines and dispositions, his case offers a striking variant on the typical plot of disadvantage. For this self maker was black in a situation where race was a source of arbitrary social limitation, the post–Civil War American South. The most interesting story these pages tell is of what happens to the nineteenth-century self-made man when that man is black and his America is racially discriminatory. The journal exhibits a character of immense talent trying to attain the knowledge and careers that his culture marks as the highest of human aspirations in a situation that distinguishes among humans on grounds other than talent—and limits access to cultural goods on those other grounds.

Charles Chesnutt's parents, free blacks descended from the group called old order free Negroes (though both also had white ancestry), came from Fayetteville, North Carolina. In the late 1850s they moved north to Cleveland to escape the oncoming Civil War, and Charles Chesnutt was born in Ohio in 1858.

But after the war the family returned to Fayetteville, which remained Chesnutt's home throughout his journal years. At first glance, postbellum Fayetteville appears to have been a fairly impoverished cultural milieu. A county seat with a population of four or five thousand, Fayetteville was the commercial center for the inland region using the Cape Fear River as its primary transportation route and the entrepôt for a local industry in pine products and naval stores. Never a bustling place, in Chesnutt's early life Fayetteville's local economy followed the general decline of the southern economy after the Confederate defeat. In what were elsewhere in America years of booming development, then, Chesnutt lived in a place well outside the centers of contemporary vitality, in a provincial town stalled in a kind of doldrums. "When I first saw the town, there brooded over it a calm that seemed almost sabbatic in its restfulness," Chesnutt's narrator says of Patesville, the fictionalized Fayetteville, in *The Conjure Woman*. A 1898 letter to Chesnutt from his old family doctor tells the since-departed native son: "The old town is very quiet still tho' we hope for better things."[1]

What Chesnutt calls "the dullness of the place" (157) was exacerbated for ambitious blacks, his journal suggests, by the racial protocols of southern society. Over and over in the journal we see Chesnutt shut out of activities that might have been sources of lively interest. The rumor reaches him at one point that Mr. Kyle, the mayor of Fayetteville, has warned Chesnutt's German teacher not to give him lessons unless he is prepared to lose his white pupils as a result. At another point Chesnutt laments: "I live in a town where there is *some* musical culture; I have studied and practiced till I can understand and appreciate good music, but I never hear what little there is to be heard" (92–93)—an exclusion again clearly based on his being marked a "nigger." At another point he is urged to withdraw from a local political contest by white well-wishers—"friends" willing to have the likes of Chesnutt in prominent segregated social positions but not in places of general civic power.

Chesnutt describes himself at one point as "cut off from

1. Charles W. Chesnutt, *The Conjure Woman and Other Conjure Tales*, Richard H. Brodhead, ed. (Durham: Duke University Press, 1993), 32. Dr. T. D. Haigh's 1898 letter to Chesnutt is in the Charles Waddell Chesnutt Papers, Special Collections, Fisk University Library.

all intercourse with cultivated society, and from almost every source of improvement" (142), and there is some truth to this self-portrait—enough so that one use of the journal is to show the local, daily forms in which postbellum racial discrimination was experienced by a highly intelligent southern black. But in a sense the interest of the journal is that it shows Chesnutt *not* cut off from every "source of improvement" but rather given access to some sources as he is denied it to others. Dull though it may appear in general outlines, the Fayetteville pictured in the journal is never anything less than a real experiential world, a fully functional, fully variegated social organism equipped—like all social settings—with its own array of local features and opportunities. Chesnutt's world may not be New York or Washington (the places he thinks of as the Metropolis), but it has its own range of cultural institutions, not all of them equally observant of the color line. Chesnutt's journal supplies material for a list of the cultural activities available to a nineteenth-century small-town black, a list that would include cross-racial temperance societies, theater clubs, African-American religious revivals, European language tutorials, teachers' meetings with black and white educators, and a great many others. Similarly, if Chesnutt lived in a small world generally organized around black-white racial difference, his journal shows that that world contained a full complement of social groupings, each placing itself in a somewhat different relation to Chesnutt and offering him a different degree of access to its cultural resources. Chesnutt was a fellow townsman, we learn, of a poor white clerk named John McLaughlin, who was convinced that however well educated Chesnutt was, he was still "a nigger; and with me a nigger is a nigger" (161)—a precursor, perhaps, of Captain McBane, the lower-class white racist Chesnutt studies in *The Marrow of Tradition*. But Fayetteville also has a white doctor who sympathizes with Chesnutt's social proscriptions; a bookseller from the same elite family who holds strict conservative beliefs in race and class barriers yet opens his bookstore to Chesnutt and converses with surprising candor; a European-educated Yankee merchant lured to postwar Fayetteville by the naval stores business who joins Chesnutt in temperance activities and study; and a German Jewish intellectual, the newly arrived immigrant relative of a local German Jewish merchant, who teaches Chesnutt languages against the counsel of well-placed whites, partly out of the sympathy of one victim of prejudice for the plight of another.

But the greatest cultural opportunity that Fayetteville made available to Chesnutt lay in the school it provided for blacks. The Howard School, a free public grade school for black children, was established at Fayetteville in 1867. Like all social institutions, it was created through the confluence of more general historical forces, forces in this case especially interesting and complex. The Howard School was enabled in the most primary way by the Civil War and the abolition of slavery, since before 1865 it was illegal to educate blacks in slave states. The school was further enabled by the surge of northern philanthropic activity just after emancipation, a drive to undo the freed slaves' forced inferiorization that took education as its chief remedy. The Howard School was erected with the support of the Freedman's Bureau, a short-lived federal agency set up during Reconstruction to promote the social welfare of emancipated slaves. (The school has this historical connection written into its name: it was named for General O. O. Howard, the vigorous leader of the Freedman's Bureau, later a founder and the head of Howard University.) The nongovernmental philanthropies of this time assisted the school as well. Its first teacher and leader—Robert Harris, like Chesnutt's parents a Fayetteville-born free black who had migrated to Cleveland before the war—was sponsored by the American Missionary Society, one of the many church-based agencies active in freedmen's education in the postwar years. It also drew support from the Peabody Educational Fund, the million-dollar trust established by the financier George Peabody (founder of what became the House of Morgan) to further free public education in the South.

But if it had white northern help, the Howard School also took form through the efforts of southern blacks, efforts again highly characteristic of the late 1860s and early 1870s. As many sources have established, the fact that literate education was forbidden to slaves had the unintended effect of making this education appear a fundamental human necessity, the very embodiment of freedom and empowerment, to those refused its benefits. The passionate esteem for education paradoxically produced by its withholding fueled another of the great dramas of the postbellum South, blacks' massive drive to learn to read and write. We find one testimony to this urge in Chesnutt's contemporary Booker T. Washington's memory of his "intense longing to learn to read," the longing that drove him to "walk several miles at night" after a long day of labor "in order to recite my night-school lessons." We find another testimony in William Pickens's account of how his parents—once illiterate slaves—moved their family from country to town in order to get better schooling for their children, and reorganized their family economy so as to free the children to study. The Howard School in Fayetteville is one more embodiment of the historical determination by blacks (in Washington's words) "to secure an education at any cost." If the Freedman's Bureau built the school building, seven local Negroes—one of them Chesnutt's father—bought the lots on Gillespie Street on which the school was built. The $136 they paid, like the labor they lost when their children attended the school, represented the sacrifice they were willing to incur to gain the good of literate education.[2]

Fayetteville's Howard School is a representative development in postbellum black education in terms of the forces that helped establish it. But social forces work themselves out differently in different local settings, and it should be emphasized that the

2. Of the many sources relevant to the history of the Howard School, Robert C. Morris's *Reading, 'Riting, and Reconstruction: The Education of Freedmen in the South, 1861–1870* (Chicago: University of Chicago Press, 1981) might be cited as a general consideration of white philanthropic efforts. James D. Anderson's *The Education of Blacks in the South, 1860–1935* (Chapel Hill: University of North Carolina Press, 1988) makes the strongest case for the action of southern blacks on their own educational behalf, on pp. 4–32 especially. Constance E. H. Daniel, "Two North Carolina Families—the Harrises and the Richardsons," *Negro History Bulletin* 13 (October 1949): 3–12; and Earle H. West, "The Harris Brothers: Black Northern Teachers in the Reconstruction South," *Journal of Negro Education* 48 (1979): 126–38, are useful sources on Robert Harris, as is Chesnutt's obituary of Harris, printed in the *Catalogue of the North Carolina State Colored Normal School, Fayetteville, N.C., for the Year 1880–81* (Fayetteville: J. E. Garrett, 1881), 18–19. Quotations from Booker Washington come from *Up from Slavery* (1901; rpt., New York: Penguin Books, 1986), 27 and 37, but his whole chapter "Boyhood Days" is relevant to this discussion. So is William Pickens's 1911 autobiography, *The Heir of Slaves*, included in the enlarged volume *Bursting Bonds* (1923), recently edited and introduced by William L. Andrews (Bloomington: Indiana University Press, 1991).

general processes I have been describing produced something quite particular in postwar Fayetteville: not just a school for blacks but one of the most notable schools in the state. Historically, the fact that the Howard School was a free public grade school (graded school, in the nineteenth-century idiom) is not an irrelevant piece of information. The elementary school open universally, without charge, in which well-trained teachers teach students broken into progressive grades is the most everyday of realities in the twentieth century, but it was still a relatively new idea in mid-nineteenth-century America. Promoted by the Massachusetts-based Horace Mann and others in the 1830s and 1840s, the graded school represented the most modern school model of its time; and if this model had been widely implemented in the Northeast by 1865, it was still little adopted in the South. The work of northern educators on behalf of the freed slaves helped carry this model to the former slave states. In consequence, the school system marked advanced was instituted in black education in Fayetteville before it was adopted in white schools.

Because it was so well run, this school, already advantaged in its progressive educational plan, won the further advantage of strong financial backing. To grasp the uniqueness of the Howard School it is important to remember how ill-supported North Carolina schools were in the postbellum years. Black schools had to be created from scratch, and often had to scrape together resources from the poorest section of the population. But white schools too were poorly funded at this time—especially after 1870, when the state supreme court ruled unconstitutional the property-tax mechanism by which public schools were to be supported.[3] The Howard School's relation to the Peabody Fund takes on its meaning against this background. Rather than dribbling its funds away in small gifts to many schools of marginal strength, the Peabody Fund proposed to support a few schools that were (in its phrase) "well-regulated," on the idea that they could set an example for others in the state. The fact that the Howard School fit this category meant that it received a lion's share of the Peabody Fund support—in

3. For helpful information, see Edgar W. Knight, *Public School Education in North Carolina* (Boston: Houghton Mifflin, 1916), 238–49.

the 1870s, nearly one-third of the total awarded to black schools in the whole of North Carolina.[4]

Two facts suggest the extreme prestige that attached to this well-managed, well-financed school in the 1870s. First, when the movement to introduce grade schools to white education caught on in North Carolina in the late 1870s, it was led by Alexander Graham, a white teacher from Fayetteville who was trying to match the quality of the black schooling in his town. (The city fathers are reported to have asked Graham to create white graded schools for Fayetteville after the embarrassment of a court trial at which five white boys had to make their marks while six black boys signed their names with ease.)[5] Second, when the state of North Carolina decided to create state-supported normal schools for the training of white and black teachers in 1877 (another belated imitation of the educational practices of the Northeast), it chose Fayetteville's Howard School to become the state's colored normal school.

I may seem to have made a long detour into the remote reaches of educational history, but this history is essential to the journal that follows. The availability of the Howard School was the most decisive fact of Charles Chesnutt's early life. It would scarcely be possible to overstate the extent to which the character recorded in this journal is a creature of his school. By the time the journal begins Chesnutt is already a prize graduate of the Howard School. He has already gone on to the work that such a prize pupil might expect: he is the assistant teacher at the Peabody School at Charlotte, the other black North Carolina school heavily funded by the Peabody Educational Fund, working under Cicero Harris, the brother of his Fayetteville teacher Robert Harris (so small is the world, or so tight the network, of

4. For relevant background, see ibid., 271–92. Knight's data show Peabody funds being apportioned as follows in 1875: "a negro school at Charlotte, $600; one at Fayetteville and one at Tarboro, $450 each" (286); and in 1876, "a negro school at Fayetteville and one at Charlotte, $450 each; a negro school at Tarboro and one at Raleigh, $300 each" (287). As Knight's figures show, Peabody funds were allocated both more widely and more generously to white North Carolina schools in the same years.

5. This story, supplied to the author by Graham, appears in M. C. S. Noble, *A History of the Public Schools of North Carolina* (Chapel Hill: University of North Carolina Press, 1930), 403. The white boys had had access only to an eight-week public school, while the Howard School ran for the full school year.

high-level black education in 1870s North Carolina). No less significantly, in his spare time the young Chesnutt hangs out at his
teachers' homes—his family home is scarcely mentioned here—
and elaborately emulates their ways. In his leisure time he reads
the books his teachers read: books with titles as unappetizing
to the nonprofessional educator as *The Theory and Practice of
Teaching, The Means and Ends of Universal Education,* and *School
Economy. A Treatise of the Preparation, Organization, Employments,
Government, and Authorities of Schools.* (Many of these texts were
donated to North Carolina schools by a publisher working co-
operatively with the Peabody Fund, the route by which they
came into Chesnutt's hands.)[6] In his free time he also writes in
his journal, in imitation of Cicero Harris. Or he sets himself
self-enforced homework assignments, making himself teacher
and student in one.

The founding of a virtual flagship school for blacks in his
hometown in the very years when he reached school age gave
Chesnutt, by pure biographical coincidence, extremely unusual
educational opportunities. Because of his connection with this
milieu, his journal provides an almost unique record of the daily
actualities of black schooling in the postbellum years. The journal gives a wonderfully detailed image of the quite different
world of black rural education that existed alongside the one
Chesnutt was trained in. During Reconstruction, the same compulsion to obtain withheld knowledge that led black families in
Fayetteville to build the Howard School led the much larger
mass of black agricultural laborers to try to provide schooling
for their children too, within the constraints of their lower in-
comes and less leisured lives. The primitive schools established
by blacks in country districts have been memorialized briefly in
William Pickens's *Heir of Slaves,* and at length and with intricate
nostalgia in W. E. B. Du Bois's *Souls of Black Folk.* But Chesnutt's journal describes such schools at first hand, as they are
experienced by someone spending the day inside them.[7]

6. Knight lists the elementary texts donated to North Carolina schools by northern publishers in *Public School Education in North Carolina,* 278. The list sub-
stantially overlaps with the list of textbooks Chesnutt mentions reading in his
journal.
7. For memoirs of rural schools, see Pickens, *Bursting Bonds,* 5–6; and W. E. B.
Du Bois, "The Meaning of Progress," in *The Souls of Black Folk, Writings* (New

In the first journal especially, which is largely an account of Chesnutt's hunt for summer jobs during the vacation of the Peabody School in his sixteenth and seventeenth years (1874–75), we get an extraordinarily vivid impression of how this more primitive world looks to a black youth of more sophisticated, town-bred schooling. Searching for work in Jonesville (or Jonahsville), North Carolina, in the hinterland near Charlotte—though "where the 'ville' was I am not able to say, for there was but one house within nearly half a mile of the 'church'" (60)—Chesnutt registers the sort of material conditions a country school might be held in, a dilapidated log church with no windows, plentiful cracks in the walls, and "a lamp without a chimney suspended to the joists by a string" (60). His account of his 1875 summer job in the country outside Spartanburg, South Carolina, gives a similarly evocative record both of a country teacher's joys and miseries in his school and of his life outside it—a life spent "boarding 'round" with his pupils' families, noting their curious ways and trying to get them to come up with his pay.[8]

As it evokes the practices of rural black schooling, the journal also affords a glimpse into the potential clash of outlooks between education bringers and their patrons that this situation embodied. At the end of his Jonesville job hunt Chesnutt has

York: Library of America, 1986), 405–14. Such schools take on great symbolic importance as workplaces for educated blacks in two important African-American novels of the later nineteenth century: Frances E. W. Harper's *Iola Leroy, or Shadows Uplifted* (1892) and Chesnutt's *The House behind the Cedars* (1900). The most thorough history of rural southern schooling, white and black, can be found in William A. Link, *A Hard Country and a Lonely Place: Schooling, Society, and Reform in Rural Virginia, 1870–1920* (Chapel Hill: University of North Carolina Press, 1986).

8. Though Chesnutt does not note it, these practices characterized both rural black schooling and the older national model of schooling which the professionalized grade school was superseding. Edward Eggleston's 1870 novel *The Hoosier Schoolmaster* portrays a situation much like Chesnutt's here, a community-controlled one-room school whose teacher is paid partly by being given board. But Eggleston remembers this as a past feature of rural Indiana, something still available to memory but since thoroughly reformed. Part of the meaning of rural backwardness in the late nineteenth-century South, Chesnutt's journal suggests, is that an obsolete education system already nostalgically recollected in the North was still in use in this social zone.

dinner with a black country family, then enters into a conversation that must often have taken place but that we have little
historical access to except through this record: "After supper
we had a talk concerning schools[,] schoolteachers and preachers. The old man said that 'you preachers and teachers are too
hard on us. You want us to pay you thirty or forty dollars a
month for sitting in the shade, and that is as much as we can
make in 2 or 3 months.' I tried to convince him that we earned
it, but he couldn't see the point" (61). In this scene Chesnutt's
usual monologue opens out to incorporate the viewpoint of
someone profoundly different in social position. Through this
dialogue the presumptions of the educated young professional
are exposed to the criticisms of his rustic antithesis, a client un-
persuaded that Chesnutt's rather mysterious services are worth
their high cost or even that what he does is actually work. (From
the point of view of a farm laborer, teaching may indeed seem
like high-paid idleness, "sitting in the shade.") When Chesnutt
tries to argue that his interlocutor can easily afford a teacher
or preacher but is just being cheap, he provokes a stronger
clarification of the old man's position:

> "Well, I think it's a bad chance if you can't afford to give
> your elder ten cents apiece twice a year!"
> "Well, but we haven't got any chance. We all of [us]
> work on other people's, white people's, land, and some-
> times get cheated out of all we make; and we can't get the
> money." (61–62)

The rural black who distrusts the teacher's value reveals himself
here as a sharecropper, a freedman caught in the new peon-
age of tenant farming. This fact, the man's specific economic
position, explains why he feels he can't afford education's costs.
But facing his client's situation lets the young teacher impro-
vise a new justification for his expensive services: namely, that
education will give such people the tools to combat their vic-
timization, its short-term cost being offset by the release from
economic entrapment it might help them achieve. "Now, I'll tell
you. You say you are all renters, and get cheated out of your
labor, why dont you send your children to school, and qualify
them to look out for themselves, to own property, to figure and

think about what they are doing, so that they may do better than you?" (62).

Chesnutt's journal offers a vantage point from which to look out at the educational landscape of the postbellum period—a landscape where formal education is still a relatively scarce commodity and its value still a subject of debate. But the journal affords a no less interesting look within, inside the specialized kind of self Chesnutt's educational milieu helped form. In this conversation, as in many others, Chesnutt feels distanced from southern rural blacks, whom he thinks of as fundamentally different from himself. What makes the difference between them is, precisely, his education, his command of school-taught knowledge. In his job in "the woods" (68) Chesnutt finds that he pronounces his vowels one way, in the "correct" Standard English taught in schools, and his pupils another, with the accent of the local vernacular. His relation to educated language makes him see his pupils as "they," not the equally possible "we." After school Chesnutt enjoys the poetry of Byron and Cowper while his hosts work the farm. Here again school-formed reading habits make him behave differently from his rural fellows, and so make him seem to *be* a different sort of person.

But it is not his relation to language alone that gives Chesnutt his sense of identity. One thing Chesnutt's journal makes emphatically clear is that literacy was not dispensed by itself in the sort of school he frequented. In these schools language arts were embedded in a distinctive literate culture, such that to learn these arts was to learn a whole world of related practices and values as well. The first pages of the journal are illuminating here. On his second day of journal keeping the adolescent Chesnutt dutifully copies a series of paragraphs from a book called *A Handbook for Home Improvement.* These solemnly recited guidelines for proper bathing, the prevention of foot odor, proper nail care, and changing underwear may strike modern readers as amusing, but in fact they present a serious historical exhibit of the relation of education to acculturation in the mid-nineteenth century. What Chesnutt is rehearsing, with the aid of a printed manual, are the rules of a civilization either sufficiently foreign to him or sufficiently important for him to master that he consciously formulates its otherwise unspoken laws. (Civilizations, Norbert Elias reminds us, have as their elemental structure the prescription of bodily decorum.)[9] The cultural system Chesnutt is mastering here has clearly marked social origins in nineteenth-century America. This fetishistic attention to physical decency was a specialized property of the nineteenth-century middle class, a group that had privileged access to the means to cleanliness at a time when plumbing and laundry facilities were not universal possessions and that made bodily propriety one base of its self-esteem. These rules also played out at the level of physical decency the attitude of selfhood that is the deepest mark of nineteenth-century bourgeois culture: the sense that the self exists to control itself, to remake itself through a strong action of inward regulation.[10]

The middle class that emerged in the Northeast in the mid-nineteenth century was the group that pressed for the public graded school, which was designed to impart this culture of self-discipline along with its more specific instruction.[11] Not surprisingly, then, when postwar philanthropists carried this northern scheme of schooling to southern blacks, they more or less consciously carried the northern middle-class culture of self-control with it. Fisk University inspected student rooms for neatness as it imparted higher education, and required a twice-weekly bath. Booker T. Washington, the great advocate of the daily bath and the well-used toothbrush, learned a meticulous standard of cleanliness under the tutelage of Mrs. Viola Ruffner, the " 'Yankee' woman from Vermont" who also taught him the value of a library.[12] Chesnutt too met this otherwise

9. Norbert Elias, *The Civilizing Process,* trans. Edmund Jephcott (New York: Urizen Books, 1978).

10. For a valuable history of the nineteenth-century middle-class culture of self-control, see Mary P. Ryan, *The Cradle of the Middle Class: The Family in Oneida County, New York, 1790–1865* (Cambridge: Cambridge University Press, 1981), especially chapters 2 and 4. Susan Warner's mid-nineteenth-century best-seller *The Wide, Wide World* gives a splendid exhibit of the cults of self-discipline and of bodily decency conjoined in the middle-class world of this time.

11. On the mid-nineteenth-century public school and its civilizing program, see Stanley K. Schultz, *The Culture Factory: Boston Public Schools, 1789–1860* (New York: Oxford University Press, 1973); and my "Sparing the Rod: Discipline and Fiction in Antebellum America," *Representations* 21 (1988): 67–96.

12. Washington, *Up from Slavery,* 43–45. Morris cites Fisk's emphasis on "the most scrupulous neatness" (160) in his useful discussion of the "civilizing" mission of northern-sponsored black schools in *Reading, 'Riting, and Reconstruction,* 149–60.

foreign culture in the northern-based school milieu. (It is telling that he encountered *A Handbook of Home Improvement* at the home of his northern-trained teacher.) And part of what it meant for him to become a star pupil was that he took this culture deep inside him: became the kind of self this system prescribed.

The marks Chesnutt's school acculturation put on his character are evident on every page of the journal. In leisure, his invariable idea of how to use his freedom is to plan some strenuous self-improvement—to teach himself two or three foreign languages, or to increase his already formidable speed at shorthand, or to invent an improvement for the organ. When he begins teaching, he presumes that his task is both to reeducate others in the proper use of English and to remake their characters. Under his management the Fayetteville Colored Normal School had two student organizations, a literary society and a temperance society based on the principle of total abstinence;[13] later entries in the journal make clear that he also tried to teach the control of other fleshly appetites, to impart a norm of sexual continence not familiar to his charges. The whole of this learned culture, and not education narrowly conceived, forms the base of his sense of difference from others. When uneducated rural blacks seem (as they always do) profoundly *other* to this writer, the outlook he has taken in through his schooling organizes his sense of difference. Chesnutt writes, for instance, of his South Carolina hosts:

> Well! uneducated people, are the most bigoted, superstitious, hardest headed people in the world! Those folks down stairs believe in ghosts, luck, horse shoes, cloud signs and all other kinds of nonsense, and all the argument in the world couldn't get it out of them. It is useless to argue with such persons. All the eloquence of a Demosthenes, the logic of Plato, the demonstrations of the most learned men in this world, couldn't convince them of the falsity, the absurdity, the utter impossibility and unreasonableness of

13. The Normal Band of Hope, as it was called, was founded by Robert Harris and required students to pledge to "abstain from the use of intoxicating drinks, from the use of tobacco in any form, and from all profane and vulgar language" (West, "The Harris Brothers," 132).

14

such things. Verily, education is a great thing, and I would
I could quote a quire or two of Mayhew's Universal Education on the subject, "Education lessens and dissipates the
effects of ignorance."[14] (81–82)

Chesnutt is thinking in class terms here, so it may be appropriate to note that what he himself exemplifies is a relatively new
class phenomenon of the later nineteenth century. In each of his
deepest personal devotions—to self-discipline and hard work,
to higher learning, and to using formal education to counter
the blight of ignorance—Chesnutt exemplifies a group coming
to social identity in the postbellum decades that can variously
be labeled the black intelligentsia, the black bourgeoisie, or
the black professional class. Already by his mid-teens Chesnutt
is a full-blown representative of what W. E. B. Du Bois later
called the "talented tenth,"[15] the educated elite that emerged

14. Strikingly, it is the graded reader, essential instrument of the nineteenth-
century grade school, that serves to organize others into hierarchical social
grades in this passage's thought. Chesnutt continues: "The people down stairs
don't know words enough for a fellow to carry on conversation with them. He
must reduce his phraseology several degrees lower than that of the first reader,
and then all the reason and demonstration has no more effect that a drop of
water on a field of dry wheat!" (82).

15. Du Bois uses this phrase in the chapter "On the Training of Black Men"
in *The Souls of Black Folk*, 435, and he elaborates on it in his essay "The Talented Tenth," *Writings*, 842–61. Du Bois primarily has black college graduates
in mind—still a very small contingent in 1903 when he wrote these pieces, but a
group that had grown sharply since 1885. Before that date, as in Chesnutt's case,
a much lower level of formal schooling would have marked the educated caste.

Frenise A. Logan's survey of black professionals makes clear both how small
a fraction this group formed of the late nineteenth-century black population
and how heavily weighted the black professional class was toward preachers
and teachers. By Logan's count the 1890 North Carolina census lists 2036
blacks—considerably less than 0.5 percent of the black population—in professional positions, 1940 of them (95 percent) clergymen or teachers. (The other
jobs the census categorizes as professional service are lawyers, government offi-
cials, physicians and surgeons, and artists—groups dividing among them the
remaining 94 black census registrants.) See Logan, *The Negro in North Carolina,
1876–1894* (Chapel Hill: University of North Carolina Press, 1964), 105–16.

Matthew Leary Perry, a Negro physician of Fayetteville in the twentieth
century, has cataloged the black professionals who eventually emerged from
Chesnutt's town, which was, he suggests, a strong center of black professional-
class formation. See Perry, "The Negro in Fayetteville," in John A. Oates, ed.,
The Story of Fayetteville (Raleigh: Dowd Press, 1957), 705–15.

as a leadership cadre in postemancipation black society; and this class's social formation is what Chesnutt's personal journal helps uncover. The figures who composed this group—doctors, lawyers, preachers, and especially educators—were taught in the new schools that arose with the end of slavery, and so were enabled by an education like Chesnutt's. But they were also reacculturated in those schools: steeped in an ethos of self-discipline and achievement at first located elsewhere. A white northern ethic became a southern black possession through the agency of the new schools. But this possession was not acquired without producing a change in social identity. The education that equipped some blacks to assume leadership positions in the project of uplifting the illiterate masses also tended to make them experience themselves as different *from* the masses. Chesnutt would later study this paradox with painful acuteness in the novel *The Marrow of Tradition,* but at the time of his journals he does not yet know it as an abstract social fact. Instead he shows this cadre's more general process of self-differentiation working itself out as if in merely individual terms, in the establishment of one person's sense of self and world.

Chesnutt's first journal ends in 1875. By the time his second journal begins, in the fall of 1877, important changes have taken place in his situation. In the public sphere, this interval marks the end of official Reconstruction, a fact marked in North Carolina by the sweeping of the Republican party from power in 1876. Paradoxically, the defeat of the party that blacks overwhelmingly supported was followed by an advance in state-aided black education, an advance that made a crucial difference for Chesnutt. In 1877 the North Carolina legislature voted to establish two state normal schools for the training of teachers, one for whites and one for blacks, and appropriated $2000 of state funds for each school. The white normal school was established within the University of North Carolina at Chapel Hill. After an inspection visit by the governor, the state elected to elevate the Howard School in Fayetteville into the colored normal school, with Robert Harris serving as its first principal.[16]

16. On the selection of the site for the State Colored Normal School, see Noble, *History of the Public Schools of North Carolina,* 422–23.

Beginning in the fall of 1877, the State Colored Normal School at Fayetteville offered a three-year course of study that certified its graduates as teachers of the highest grade. The only such institution in the state, this school offered free tuition, books, and travel expenses to youths "of good moral character" who could "pass a good examination in easy reading, spelling, writing, and the fundamentals of arithmetic."[17] Universal history, physiology, astronomy, algebra, bookkeeping, grammar, geography, dictation, composition, oratory, and manners and morals were offered in the third year of this training, which took place on the second story of the Howard School building. In exchange for this education, the pupils had to pledge to teach for at least three years after graduating.

Chesnutt was appointed Robert Harris's assistant in the State Colored Normal School when it was founded in 1877. In consequence, the Chesnutt of the second journal has made a meteoric rise into the top ranks of black educators in the state. (He became the principal of the normal school in 1880, at the age of twenty-two.) He raises the level of his personal study program at this time as well. More a homework notebook than a diary, his 1877–78 journal shows him patiently laboring to furnish himself with the knowledge of ancient history and Latin and French, systematically storing his mind with classical literature and the best approved theory of rhetoric (Hugh Blair's). Chesnutt's already well-developed habits of self-improvement have intensified, by this point, into a virtual compulsion. Leisure is hateful to the author of these pages, an evil to be redeemed only by the most systematic efforts to turn free time to profit. At this stage Chesnutt finds profit above all in the liberal arts, whose study he pursues with the intentness of an addict.

The spectacle of a person with ferocious will using self-devised means to *learn* as Chesnutt does here will seem at once strange and familiar to those who have had higher education provided for them as a matter of course. What Chesnutt is trying to accomplish is more or less consciously to put himself through college, to give himself a college education in the absence of a college. One of the by-products of this effort is that it generates a new and growing consciousness of the meaning of

17. Ibid., 423.

his social position, a sharp sense of his exclusion from deeply longed for cultural resources. The conscientious studies of the second journal are punctuated at one point by an extraordinary passage, which understands mandatory self-education as the flip side of blocked access to institutions of higher learning. (The painful solitude Chesnutt's campaign of self-instruction imposed on him comes clear here as well):

> I do not think that I will ever forget my Latin. The labor I spend in trying to understand it thoroughly, and the patience which I am compelled to exercise in clearing up the doubtful or difficult points, furnishes[,] it seems to me, as severe a course of mental discipline as a college course would afford. I would above all things like to enjoy the ~~privilege~~ advantages of a good school, but must wait for a future opportunity.
> —In some things I seem to be working in the dark. I have to feel my way along, but by perseverance I manage to make better headway than many who have the light; and besides, like the Edmund Dantes in Dumas' "Monte Cristo," I have become accustomed to the darkness. As I have been thrown constantly on my own resources in my solitary study, I have acquired some degree of *self-reliance*. As I have no learned professor or obliging classmate to construe the hard passages, and work the difficult problems, I have *"persevered"* till I solved them myself. (92)

The all-American virtue of self-reliance, this passage ruefully notes, is doubly needed by some Americans. And Chesnutt's next words show his new awareness that his lack of personal opportunity is social in cause: "As to procuring instruction in Latin, French, German, or Music, that is entirely out of the question. First class teachers would not teach a 'nigger' and I would have no other sort" (93).

As Chesnutt becomes aware of the arbitrary racial system that enforces it on him, self-education becomes a more and more melancholy project; his efforts to increase his personal powers always remind him of the social fact of his deprivation. When, in a kind of dream come true, a visiting northern educator tests Chesnutt on his self-taught Latin and praises his achievements, the confirmation of his success both elates him and opens an "old sore" (105), the bitter consciousness of his exclusion on grounds of race. As the sense of his situation grows on him, Chesnutt begins to use his diary to project another life for himself, to think his way out of the racially discriminatory local scene and to imagine a self not circumscribed by its prejudice. As he enters his twenties the tense of his journal becomes increasingly the future tense, the tense of things that are not now but yet will be. "I *will* go to the North," "I *will* live down the prejudice, I *will* crush it out," "I *will* show to the world that a man may spring from a race of slaves, and yet far excel many of the boasted ruling race," "I *will* test the social problem. I *will* see if it's possible for talent, wealth, genius to acquire social standing and distinction" (93, 106; my italics), he writes with strident iteration in the powerful journal entries of 1879–81. In these passages journal writing becomes an act of resolution building, a place to exercise the powers of will and hope necessary to create another life.

In keeping with this aim, Chesnutt begins to use his journal to envision the other careers that might await him and the paths that might lead him to them. "I guess I'll study for a Doctor. I must work, save money, study as hard as I can, till I'm ready, pocket and mind to enter a Med. Coll., and go to read in some Doc's Office" (74), the future-achievement-oriented Chesnutt is already writing at age seventeen. Later he has another idea: "I will go to the Metropolis, or some other large city, and like Franklin[,] Greely and many others, there will I stick. . . . I depend principally upon my knowledge of stenography, which I hope will enable me to secure a position on the staff of some good newspaper, and then,—work, work, work!" (106). (His record of his 1879 scouting trip to Washington, D.C., and of his exploration of the career opportunities for educated blacks in that urban cultural and political center is one of the most fascinating entries in the second journal.)

Among the other careers he entertains, the career of the writer figures especially prominently among Chesnutt's aspirations: "It is the dream of my life—to be an author!" (154). His will to write has deep foundations in his schooling, which strongly promoted the value both of written literacy in general and of literary achievement in particular. (Chesnutt's self-conscious first attempt at literary writing, the sketch "Lost in a

Swamp" printed below, is devised in the image of a school exercise, an assigned "theme.") The will to write has the quality of a deep inward impulse to Chesnutt, who says at one point: "I feel an influence that I cannot resist calling me to the task" (139). But by his twenties Chesnutt thinks of writing largely as a way *out,* a way to achieve a selfhood not bounded by his local scene. In a 1881 inventory of available careers Chesnutt marks writing as the other career open to the well-schooled yet unfunded, "the only thing I can do without capital, under my present circumstances, except teach" (154–55). This great aspirer continues his examination of his prospects:

> I want fame; I want money; I want to raise my children in a different rank of life from that I sprang from. In my present vocation, I could never accumulate a competency, with all the economy and prudence, and parsimony in the world. In law or medicine, I would be compelled to wait half a life-time to accomplish anything. But literature pays—the successful. . . . My three month vacation is before me after the lapse of another three, and I shall strike for an entering wedge in the literary world, which I can drive in further afterwards. (154–55)

Chesnutt's journal displays the immense idealism that he brought to the literary calling, which he saw as another way of furthering his race's cause. But more practical desires—above all the need for worldly success—figure in Chesnutt's literary ambitions as well. In keeping with this worldly orientation, when Chesnutt thinks about writing as a career he always pays careful attention to the places where his writing could be brought to public life, and to the self-presentation that would make his work suitable to such places. In the letter drafted for the *Christian Union,* for instance, Chesnutt tests out the persona he hopes will make him a desirable correspondent for that liberal northern journal. In this unsuccessful early effort at publication he projects the carefully constructed image of himself as a southern colored man (his revisions show that at first he posed as white) of appropriately liberal intelligence: the reasonable decrier of "unreasonable prejudice" (107), the idealistic advocate of a postracial "New American Nation" (108), who reassures his northern hearers that racial progress is advancing in the South and that southern blacks only want greater opportunities to join "the influential 'middle class'" (108) and make private property secure.

The lack of literary centers in the South meant that Chesnutt's ambition to write always drove him mentally northward, the North being the place where a literary career could be successfully established in his time. And it was by studying the operation of northern literary markets, the journal makes clear, that Chesnutt came to discover black southern life as a possible literary subject. The best-seller reception of *A Fool's Errand,* the fictional history of Reconstruction in North Carolina by the former carpetbagger Albion Tourgée, is of riveting interest to Chesnutt in the spring of 1880. This book's highly visible success brings him two revelations: first, that southern blacks and the complications of their postemancipation history are of literary interest "to the Northern mind" (125); and, second, that for this reason, he might be able to establish himself as a writer by recording the racial history that surrounds him. Falling into the mood of sublime self-dedication that is his journal's increasingly common tone, Chesnutt finds a calling for himself in Tourgée's example:

And if Judge Tourgee, with his necessarily limited intercourse with colored people, and with his limited stay in the South, can write such interesting descriptions, such vivid pictures of Southern life and character as to make himself rich and famous, why could not a colored man, who has lived among colored people all his life; who is familiar with their habits, their ruling passions, their prejudices; their whole moral and social condition; their public and private ambitions; their religious tendencies and habits;— why could not a colored man who knew all this, and who, besides, had possessed such opportunities for observation and conversation with the better class of white men in the south as to understand their modes of thinking; who was familiar with the political history of the country, and especially with all the phases of the slavery question;—why could not such a man, if he possessed the same ability, write a far better book about the South than Judge Tourgee or

Mrs. Stowe has written? Answer who can! But the man is yet to make his appearance; and if I can't be the man I shall be the first to rejoice at his dèbut and give God speed! to his work. (125–26)

It is notable that Chesnutt moves straight from this meditation on Tourgée's success to a literary foraging plan of his own: a plan for collecting "things . . . which are peculiar [to the colored people and] . . . would be doubly interesting to people who know little about them" (126).

Chesnutt's first literary success was as an author of black vernacular fiction, the conjure stories printed in the *Atlantic Monthly* in the late 1880s. His journal shows that his turn specifically to southern black vernacular materials was the product of a movement out toward and back from distant literary worlds similar to what this entry records. One misapprehension Chesnutt's journal will dispel is the notion that black vernacular culture was in any simple way *his* culture. Chesnutt's schooling, the training that in the most fundamental way enabled him as a writer, was based on the systematic devaluation and even suppression of this vernacular. In the realm of language this schooling aimed to supplant locally accented, orally structured black English with Standard English based on correct writing. Robert Harris scheduled an "exercise in articulation at every recitation" at the Howard School to teach his black pupils the foreign language of literate English, "so different is their language from that in the books."[18] Chesnutt the future dialect writer spent his early years trying to break black pupils of their dialect speech: "All the scholars say 'dō,' 'thē,' 'ā,' 'ăre,' &c. which I must first 'unteach' them (if I may coin a word)" (71). The Enlightenment ethos attached to literacy in Chesnutt's schooling disparaged folk science and folk religion to a similar extent. Chesnutt's hosts in his South Carolina schooldays—"those folks down stairs [who] believe in ghosts, luck, horse shoes, cloud signs and all other kinds of nonsense"—are subscribers to what he will later know as conjure, but at this earlier time he can only see their folk beliefs as signs of barbarous benightedness: "Well! uneducated people, are the most bigoted, superstitious,

18. West, "The Harris Brothers," 136.

hardest headed people in the world!" (81). As the product of his education, Chesnutt's response to the culture of his illiterate black countrymen is usually one of estrangement, embarrassment, and an anxious attempt to guard his distance from it. The priggish young Chesnutt—eventual creator of the fictional folk character Uncle Julius—is mortified at being addressed as Uncle Chess at one point (77), and he later finds lowlife comedy, not fraternity, in being called "de Chesnutt Bro" (181). The spiritual enthusiasms of a black religious revival in 1880 fill him with fascination and repulsion.

Chesnutt's relation to illiterate southern black life is not, perhaps, ever unambivalently hostile. On the train to Washington, when he is made to sit in the same railroad car with a group of black farm laborers, Chesnutt feels his usual class difference from these "darkies," a difference organized for him through the different status level of their work, their different culture of bodily propriety (the workers are dirty and smelly), and a different system of sexual propriety ("his sister, he said, sat in his lap, though the affectionate way in which he embraced her seemed . . . to render the relationship doubtful" [112–13]). At the same time, Chesnutt feels an instinctive admiration for the joyousness of this group, whose entertainment resources—the communal, participatory singing of hymns—are so different from his own culture's preferred entertainment (silent, privatized reading).

But if he admires it on occasion, it is only when Chesnutt begins seeing black vernacular culture through the eyes of distant cultures that he begins to take a more positive interest in it. In a long journal entry in the spring of 1880 Chesnutt writes in part:

> I have thought, during the great revival which is going on, that a collection of the ballads or hymns which the colored people sing with such fervor, might be acceptable, if only as a curiosity[,] to people, literary people, at the North. Though these songs are not of much merit as literary compositions, they have certain elements of originality which make them interesting to a student of literature, who can trace, in a crude and unpolished performance, more of the natural ability or character of the writer than in the more correct production of a cultivated mind. Burns and Bun-

23

yan rank, in literature, far above many inferior authors who could manufacture polished Alexandrines and heroic couplets. (121–22)

Long before his actual work with the vernacular, Chesnutt begins here to articulate a theory of the literary value of the vernacular. But this theory is not a product of North Carolina vernacular culture, as the allusions to British authors make clear: it is created through the reconceptualization of local life within imported conceptual materials. In this passage Chesnutt's literary ambitions again drive him to pay attention to the distant world where literary reputations can be established, the world of "literary people at the North." Seeing the value literary northerners attach to black spirituals—Chesnutt would have had the success of *Slave Songs of the United States* on his mind as well as the triumphal tours of the Fisk Jubilee Singers—makes him assign a value to this local black expression that it had not possessed, for him, by itself. The demand for such work in a foreign literary economy creates Chesnutt's desire to enter into black vernacular culture. That demand establishes this culture as a commodity he can trade in, a good he can use as entry into the literary market.

With his new project in mind Chesnutt goes to work as a kind of ethnographic collector in his own hometown, sitting at the feet of a new teacher—Elder Davis, black pastor of the A.M.E. Zion church at Fayetteville—and becoming a pupil, for once, of black popular culture. In the wonderfully detailed interviews that follow, Davis helps Chesnutt to the knowledge not just of black music but of another great art form of black popular culture, preaching—as Davis makes clear, an oral art that must reach the formally *un*educated in order to succeed. This is new territory for Chesnutt, who is clearly struck by its unexpected lessons. But as he takes a new interest in a culture previously "beneath" him Chesnutt is still driven by a logic external to that culture. Like Zora Neale Hurston, whose hometown ethnography his strikingly prefigures (his interviews with Elder Davis are his versions of *Mules and Men*), Chesnutt collects an indigenous civilization with the goal of transcribing it, reprocessing it, and sending it *out* to the world that can only know it at second hand. Like Hurston, and like many other vernacular-based American authors white and black (Mark Twain would be another), Chesnutt's coming to an appreciation of this local ethos is inseparable from the process by which he strives to secure a life apart from that ethos—a life in the inevitably distant, different world of successful authors.

"I shall strike for an entering wedge in the literary world," Chesnutt had resolved in March 1881. In fact, his literary career is still several years distant when the journal ends; and the note of his last entries is not of impending success but of painfully deepening frustration. In his third journal Chesnutt has attained the peak of success available in his early world. Still in his early twenties, he is the principal of the State Colored Normal School and a person of note both in Fayetteville and throughout North Carolina. But Chesnutt shows little pleasure in his position. Instead he seems discouraged by his success, discouraged that the furthest he can go is where he is already.

It is, of course, possible that Chesnutt wrote in his journal only in withdrawn moods, and that he may have had a more engaged and fulfilling life in these years than the journal records. The journal does have conspicuous omissions: one notes the absence of references to his wife and children, his many brothers and sisters, and his fellow teachers, to name no more. But even allowing for its possible partiality, the picture that emerges here is one of striking loneliness and dejection. "Too 'stuck-up' for the colored folks" (158), Chesnutt is estranged from the black community by the superiority of his education—and no doubt by the attitude of superiority he derives *from* his education. At the same time, he is not admitted to the company of the equally educated and cultivated whites of Fayetteville, who exclude him on racial grounds. This situation is not new for Chesnutt, but it seems to have produced a new degree of misery for him by 1881, for the third journal releases an anger, bitterness, and self-pity elsewhere rare in these pages:

> I hear colored men speak of their "white friends." I have no white friends. I could not degrade the sacred name of "Friendship" by associating it with any man who feels himself too good to sit at table with me, or to sleep at the same hotel. True friendship can only exist between men who

have something in common, between equals in something, if not in everything; and where there is respect as well as admiration. I hope yet to have a friend. If not in this world, then in some distant future eon, when men are emancipated from the grossness of the flesh, and mind can seek out mind.[19] (172)

Chesnutt's anger and gloom extend to the national scene as well. The third journal shows Chesnutt attuned to the national black media of his time and well informed, through them, of the contemporary status of blacks after Reconstruction. Among other such stories, Chesnutt fixes in particular on the persecution of the early black West Point cadets Henry Ossian Flipper and Johnson Chestnut Whittaker—clearly alter egos for him because they were talented black men who had won admission to a northern college—as an index to the general hostility to black aspiration. His poem on this episode, the powerful satirical ballad "The Perplexed Nigger," is another expression of the anger that his thinking takes on at this time, anger against a racism that he knows afflicts the North as well as the South.

Chesnutt's new frustration, however, is not really a measure of defeat as much as it is the sign of an ambition that made all unfulfillment feel like defeat. That ambition drove Chesnutt beyond the point where the journal stops. The last pages of this diary are the work of a man who must get out, a man who cannot stand the restriction he lives within (the State Colored Normal School—a racially segregated school producing black teachers for a segregated school system—was, of course, a daily reminder of such restriction):[20]

19. Joel Williamson, one of the few historians who have consulted the Chesnutt journal, makes this passage a chief exhibit of the withdrawal that he sees as the characteristic black response to the separation of the races after Reconstruction; see Williamson, *The Crucible of Race: Black-White Relations in the American South since Emancipation* (New York: Oxford University Press, 1984), 65–66.

20. One of the state's reasons for wanting to provide for the training of its own colored teachers was to reduce the role of "outsiders"—liberal northerners—in the education of blacks. The Peabody Fund, it could be added, chose to support not a reconstruction-minded school system but one that would be harmonious with local interests—which meant that it effectively lent its support to segregated education.

I get more and more tired of the South. I pine for civilization and "equality." I sometimes hesitate about deciding to
go, because I am engaged in a good work, and have been
doing, I fondly hope, some little good. But many reasons
urge me the other way; and I think I could serve my race
better in some more congenial occupation. And I shudder
to think of exposing my children to the social and intellectual proscription to which I have been a victim. (172)

His rage both to achieve what his gifts enabled him to do and to
refuse any external restraint on his achievements led Chesnutt
to seek work in Washington in the summer of 1879. A surviv-
ing letter from Dr. T. D. Haigh, chairman of the white Board
of Managers of the State Colored Normal School, suggests that
he tried to relocate in New York in the summer of 1882, again
without success. But at the end of the school year in 1883 the
author of this journal resigned his post, moved first to New York
and then to Cleveland, and began pursuing the new careers
his Fayetteville years had both equipped him for and excluded
him from: lawyer and professional stenographer, business success and fully incorporated member of the professional middle
class—and author, literary recorder of postbellum southern
history.

Chesnutt's was a highly idiosyncratic life for his time and place,
and it will not do to make him out to be overly representative. Given that the black illiteracy rate still stood at 75 percent in North Carolina in 1880,[21] the very literacy of which
the journal is constant evidence differentiates Chesnutt from
the great mass of his contemporaries—the tenant farmers or
farm wage laborers glimpsed in these pages, whose very different life stories we must try to imagine. Even among his com-
parably educated contemporaries Chesnutt's life shows highly
unrepresentative turns. The more characteristic products of his
background did not leave the South or pursue careers so indi-
vidualistic as literary authorship but found their calling in education, the work Chesnutt shunned. This was the road taken by
Chesnutt's famous contemporary Booker T. Washington, whose

21. See Logan, *The Negro in North Carolina*, 140.

Tuskegee work began in 1881—and whose accommodations to the scheme of black social inferiority the author of this journal refused to make. This was also the career path of William Pickens, who returned to Talladega to teach; and, closer to home, of such Chesnutt alter egos as E. E. Smith, his successor as principal, who stayed behind and built the normal school into the Fayetteville Teachers College for Negroes; or Fayetteville's John S. Leary, the second black admitted to the North Carolina bar, founder and first dean of the Law Department of Shaw University; or Chesnutt's sister Anne, a devoted teacher and school supervisor for whom a regional high school was later named. But if it projects only one model of experience where others were equally available, Chesnutt's journal is still a striking record of a personal life formed in and against the postemancipation South's distinctive history. As well as any other document from the time, it shows the conditions that favored and those that restricted an education-loving black in the new world the abolition of slavery brought into being—and shows above all the complex self-awareness this situation helped to produce.

Robert Harris, Chesnutt's Fayetteville teacher and
superior at the State Colored Normal School

Bishop Cicero Harris, Chesnutt's superior at the
Peabody School in Charlotte

The Howard School (later the State Colored Normal
School), Fayetteville, North Carolina

Charles W. Chesnutt around 1879, aged 21

The Perry Homestead, Fayetteville, Chesnutt's wife's
family's home, where he lived from 1878 to 1880

June 27, 1883

Fayetteville N.C. June 27, 1883

Mr C. W. Chesnutt having resigned his position as Principal of the State Normal School in this place, & desiring to seek occupation in some other portion of the country,—it gives me great pleasure to testify to his good standing & moral worth & to commend him to any one who may desire his services,—as a thoroughly reliable man. a man who has thoroughly performed his duty in the position as Principal of the Normal School -giving full satisfaction to the Board of Managers & to the Patrons of the School.—His conduct as a citizen has been such as to merit & receive the approval of all & his resignation is regretted by all.

He carries with him the good wishes & commendation of our best people.

T. D. Haigh Chm. Bd Man. S.C.N.S.

Character reference given to Chesnutt by Dr. T. D. Haigh, chairman of the Board of Managers of the State Colored Normal School, upon Chesnutt's departure from Fayetteville in 1883

34

Charles Chesnutt in 1899
(the year of *The Conjure Woman*), aged 41

A NOTE ON THE TEXT

Charles Chesnutt kept a journal off and on between 1874 and his departure from the South in 1883. This journal, now in the Special Collections of the Fisk University Library in Nashville, Tennessee, consists of three volumes approximately seven by six inches in size, each with a firm cardboard cover adorned with marbled paper and a leather-covered spine. The first volume contains 160 pages, though due to a paginating error it lacks pages 132–39. The second contains 239 pages but lacks pages 184 and 185. The third has writing on 55 pages, although the last 2 pages were written significantly later (in 1885).

This edition prints the great bulk of Chesnutt's journal entries from 1874 to 1882. It does not reprint all of Chesnutt's obviously immature creative writing; some of the composition exercises he set himself in the first journal and some of his cruder attempts at poems have been omitted. On the other hand, I have been careful to retain enough examples of these genres to give a sense of the insistence of Chesnutt's writerly ambition. The other writing excerpted here involves quotations from and summaries of Chesnutt's reading. Chesnutt's journal figured prominently in his campaigns of self-education, and some parts of the journal consist of a kind of log of his studies, summarizing works Chesnutt was reading and recording impressive passages. The act of filling one's mind with learning is one of the most interesting dramas this journal records, but it is not practical to reprint all of Chesnutt's homework. Here again, a generous selection is retained to represent the journal's more extensive exercises. Eight pages of exercises in the Pittman system of shorthand have been omitted as well. With these exceptions the journals are reprinted in their entirety.

Chesnutt wrote correctly and in a clear hand, and the level of literacy he displays is one of the journal's major exhibits. Accordingly the editorial policy used in transcribing the journals has been to reprint them as they were written, with as little editorial meddling as possible. I have not corrected Chesnutt's rare misspellings and rather idiosyncratic punctuation after quotations. A certain minimal amount of punctuation has been supplied, and a missing letter or word has sometimes been added where Chesnutt's meaning would otherwise be hard to grasp, but all such additions are in brackets. Only one form of error has been silently emended: on the rare occasions when Chesnutt inadvertently wrote a word twice, the redundant duplicate has been dropped. Words written in error and then crossed out have not generally been retained, but where other word choices Chesnutt considered are of more than passing interest I have retained them with a strikethrough. Chesnutt's poems present a special case of such revision. Chesnutt often went back over his poems and wrote in alternative words and lines, letting both variants stand. In these cases both alternatives have been recorded. Other revisions of the text have been run in at the point where Chesnutt indicates they belong. The exception is a small number of entries apparently written by Chesnutt but in a later hand. These are generally reported in notes.

Authors and acquaintances mentioned by Chesnutt are annotated the first time their name appears.

FIRST JOURNAL,
1 8 7 4 – 1 8 7 5

Charlotte, Journal and Note-book
1874.

July 1. While Mr. Harris[1] was packing up to-day for his Northern trip, I came upon his journal, one which he kept several
years ago, and obtaining his permission, I have read a part of
it. In fact nearly all. After reading it, I have concluded to write
a journal too. I don't know how long I shall stick to it, but I shall
try and not give it up too soon.

Mr. Harris left this evening, on the 7 o'clock train for Fayetteville. From Fayetteville he intends to go to Cleveland, Ohio (my
birthplace). I have been teaching with him for the last 9 mos. It
is now the summer vacation, and having a First Grade Teachers
Certificate, which entitles me to (40) forty dollars a month,[2] I

1. Cicero R. Harris, the younger brother of Chesnutt's teacher Robert Harris,
had followed his brother from Cleveland to Fayetteville before moving to Charlotte, North Carolina, to become principal of the Peabody School. Chesnutt
served as assistant to Cicero Harris for three years, teaching in rural schools in
the environs of Charlotte in the summer months. Cicero Harris lived on Trade
Street in Charlotte when Chesnutt was associated with him. He later helped
found the Zion Wesley Institute (later Livingstone College), where he served as
a professor. He became a bishop of the African Methodist Episcopal [A.M.E.]
Zion church in 1889.
2. Three grades of teachers' certificates were issued in North Carolina, valid
for only one year and only in the county where they were issued. As the journal
makes clear, teachers took examinations for their certificates, which were corre-
lated with educational status and levels of pay. (Rena Walden wins a first-grade
teachers' certificate in Chesnutt's *The House Behind the Cedars*.) Forty dollars a

have concluded to stay in this country and teach during it (the vacation). I have a school 5 miles from here, on the Statesville Rail-Road. I shall begin if possible next Monday, the 5th of July. The name of the church at which I am to teach is Rockwell, and the name of the township is "Malley Creek."[3]

July 2nd. I have been reading "A Handbook for Home Improvement." Published by Fowler & Wells, New York.[4] It comprises "How to write," "How to Behave[,]" How to talk, and "How to do Business[.]" It is a very good book and I shall proceed to copy a few paragraphs.

The Daily Bath

"To keep clean you must bathe frequently. In the first place you should wash the whole body with pure soft water every morning on rising from your bed, rubbing it till dry with a coarse towel, and afterward using friction with the hands. If you have not been at all accustomed to cold bathing, commence with tepid water, lowering the temperature by degrees till that which is perfectly cold becomes agreeable. In warm weather, comfort and cleanliness alike require still more frequent bathing. Mohammed made frequent ablutions a religious duty; and in that he was right. The rank and fetid odors which exhale from a foul skin can hardly be neutralized by the sweetest incense of devotion.

The Feet

["]The feet are particularly liable to become offensively odoriferous, especially when the perspiration is profuse. Frequent washings with cold water with the occasional use of warm water and soap, are absolutely necessary to cleanliness.

---

month would have been an extraordinarily handsome salary for anyone, let alone a sixteen-year-old, in a world where black farm wage labor commanded forty cents a day.

3. Actually Mallard Creek.

4. *A Handbook for Home Improvement* is a self-help manual by Samuel Roberts Wells published around 1857. The pages in its several sections are numbered separately. Chesnutt's copyings come from the section "How to Behave" (17–18 and 29–30).

Change of Linen

"A frequent change of linen is another essential of cleanliness. It avails little to wash the body if we inclose it the next minute in soiled garments. It is not in the power of every one to wear fine and elegant clothes, but we can all, under ordinary circumstances, afford clean shirts, drawers and stockings; never sleep in any garment worn during the day; and your night[shirt] should be well aired every morning.

The nails.

"You will not, of course, go into company or sit down to the table with soiled hands, but unless you can habituate yourself to a special care of them, more or less dirt will be found lodged under your nails. Clean them carefully every time you wash your hands, and keep them smoothly and evenly cut. If you allow them to get too long, they are liable to be broken off, and become uneven and ragged, and if you pare them too closely they fail to protect the ends of the fingers."

Spitting

"The use of tobacco has made us a nation of spitters," as some one has truly remarked. Spitting is a private act, and tobacco users are not alone in violating good taste and good manners by hawking and spitting in company. You should never be seen to spit. Use your handkerchief carefully, and so as not to be noticed, or in case of necessity leave the room.

"Never pare or scrape your nails, pick your teeth, comb your hair, or perform any of the necessary operations of the toilet in company. All these things should be carefully attended to in the privacy of your own room. To pick the nose, dig the ears, or scratch the head or any part of the person in company is still worse[.] Watch yourself carefully, and if you have any such habits, break them up at once. These may seem little things, but they have their weight, and will go far in determining the character of the impression we make upon those around us."— How to Behave.

July 3rd. Yesterday evening I went up to the Section-House to complete the preparations for my school. As I stepped off the

41

car, Cap't. Johnson, one of the School Committee, got off also, and addressed me. He asked me was I not the young man who was up there looking for a school. I answered in the affirmative, and he told me that he had forgotten that those people had got money for a school-house, and that there was no money for that school. That knocked my school "higher than a kite." I went down to B. Johnson's last night to see if there was a school on his circuit. He was not at home.

9 o'clock, p.m. I went to see Mr. Johnson this morning and he said he thought I could get a school on his circuit. But alas! I hired a saddle-horse, (he cost me a dollar), and rode down to Morrow's Turnout.[5] As I crossed the boundary line between this township (Charlotte) and Pineville, I had to pass through the boundary fence, for the Fence law is in action in that township. After reaching Morrow's, I saw Mr [illegible name: Youance?], one of the school committee and he told me that all the colored schools in that Tp. were in operation. On my way back I stopped too see another of the School committee, Mr. Elliott, who was in another school district. He said there was no school house for the colored people. I returned home, paid my livery-stable bill, and here I am. I don't know what to do. I shall continue trying. As all, or nearly all the schools in Mecklenburg are filled, I think I shall try another county. I ought to make "Nil desperandum"[6] my motto.

July 6th. Saturday, the 4th of July, was the 98 anniversary of American Independence. It was a dull day here. There was nothing going on more than usual. I went up town to look around and see the country folks about a school. Got on the track of one. It was in the same township Mr. Petty was to teach in. Yesterday, Sunday, I went out to Moore's Sanctuary[7] to find of Mr. Petty who the school committee were. I waited until morning service was over, and he told me that he had lost his school, that there was but $89.93 in the treasury for that school,

5. Morrow's Turnout was the name of today's Pineville until the railroad arrived in 1852. It survived as a name for the northern part of this town just south of Charlotte.
6. "Nothing is to be despaired of; don't despair."
7. The name of an A.M.E. Zion church still active in Charlotte.

and that they were going to build a school-house with it, and that there was but $20.00 for the school I was on the track off. I started back to town about half-past 12 and got there about half-past 1 o'clock. Now, not knowing where to find a school, I have a notion of going to Raleigh, and seeing Mr. Harris[8] to find out if there [are] any schools down about home. From thence I think I shall go home; for I have got to make my living somehow, and I am not making anything, but spending all the time. I hear that William Stokes died of fever last night. He was a fine young fellow, and I am sorry, indeed.

August 10. It has been a good while since I have written any of this journal, but I will try and make amends for my fault. When I wrote the above I was about going up to Gaston Co.[9] to look for a school. I went, but got no school. I walked 23 mis. that day and when I reached town, very much fatigued, I met Mr. Harris at Grampy's. That evening I packed up and started home with Mr. H. Reached Raleigh and put up at Mr. Alston's.[10] I met Mr. Robert and Mary and Mrs. H. Mr C. R.[11] and his mother, started for Richmond at nine o'clock.

> The Old, Old Story.   July 15th 1875[12]
> Tell me the old old story,
> Of unseen things above
>   Of Jesus and his glory
>   Of Jesus and his love
> Tell me the story simply
> As to a little Child,
>   For I am weak and weary
>   And helpless and defiled.—

8. Robert Harris, Chesnutt's teacher in Fayetteville.

9. Gaston County is west of Mecklenburg County, the location of Charlotte.

10. This Mr. Alston is possibly the Reverend William J. Alston, a Raleigh native who had graduated from Oberlin and so shared a North Carolina–northern Ohio "connection" with Chesnutt and the Harrises.

11. Mr. Robert is Robert Harris, Chesnutt's Fayetteville teacher and mentor; Mary is Robert Harris's wife. Mr. C. R. is Cicero Harris.

12. A marginal note says: "The 14th and fifteenth pages of the book were skipped in 1875 [1874], and their contents are written in 1875 at Macedonia, Spartanburg Co., S.C." The pages in question comprise the four quotations reprinted here. See pp. 71–73 for journal entries contemporaneous with these copyings.

I thought I did not have this, but I have it in Pure Gold.

O the Old, Old Story! it shall be told forever,

> "And when in scenes of glory
> We sing the new, new song,
> 'Twill be the Old, old Story,
> That I have loved so long."

> "Man proud man
> Dres't in a little brief authority
> Plays such fantastic tricks before high heaven,
> As make the angels weep." [13]

> " 'Tis sweet to hear the watch-dog's honest bark,
> Bay deep mouthed welcome as we draw near home,
> 'Tis sweet to know there is an eye will mark
> Our coming and look brighter when we come;"
> *Malord's Quotation*   Byron—*Don Juan*
> Canto 1. [stanza] CXXIII

> Green grow the rashes, O!
> Green grow the rashes, O!
> The sweetest hours that e'er I spend
> Are spent among the lasses O.
> *Burns* [14]

[A further line written at the bottom of this now-crumbled page is indecipherable.—*Ed.*]

Adventure in the Capital

I staid over a day to look around and to attend the Educational Convention.[15] Attended two sessions, and heard some excel-

---

13. From Shakespeare's *Measure for Measure*, act II, scene 2.

14. The first verse of the song "Green Grow the Rashes, O!" by the Scottish poet Robert Burns (1756–1796).

15. The July 1874 gathering was the second annual convention of a group aiming to improve education in the state. Senator Augustus S. Merrimon's paper was entitled "Education in Congress." The educational issue before Congress in 1874 was school integration: in May the Senate had passed an addition to the pending Civil Rights Bill specifying that "all citizens and persons within the

lent speeches and papers read. The last time I went, to hear
Merrimon on Education[.] About the middle of this discourse,
I went out on the verandah to cool, and fell asleep on an old
sofa. When I awoke, the meeting had adjourned. I blundered
downstairs, and wandered about a good while, but reac[h]ed
Mr. Alston's at last. The next day I started for home. I arrived
at about 8 P.M., took my valise and [indecipherable line] and
the children were at home. Lilly [16] was talking very plain, and
I was surprised at her. I spent the next day (Saturday) visiting.
I "bummed" around home a week or so, and then I got the
School at Mt. Zion, [17] where I am now teaching. There was a
female, I can scarcely say lady, teaching a subscription school
out there. But when I got the public school, she got "miffed,"
and stopped a week before her term was out. She wrote me an
insulting letter, and in a few weeks she left for "Baston." She
was a sister of ———. She did not have much reputation about
here. She said she followed ——— down here, because she said
he had promised to marry her. She said she had a husband but
had left. She "cut up quite a shine" around here for awhile.
She called herself [name erased: Mary Perry.] I began to teach
Monday, 26th of July. I am getting along very well now, and
have 44 scholars, several from town. There are a few somewhat
hard cases, but I manage to manage them. I am learning to play
on the organ, at Mr. Harris'. On Thursday last, Election Day, I
acted as clerk at Rockfish Village. It is a right nice little place,
has a splendid water-power, which runs a fine factory, built of
brick. It is named "Hope Mill." I wished very much to go and
see the work, but could not, as my business would not allow me.
The Democrats gained from 5 to 15 votes at Rockfish. [18]

---

jurisdiction of the United States shall be entitled to full and equal enjoyment
of the advantages of the common schools and other institutions of learning
and benevolence without distinction of race, color, or previous condition of
servitude." The measure was tabled in the House of Representatives and never
enacted.

16. Chesnutt's sister Lillian, born in 1871. Chesnutt's mother had died after the
birth of Lilly, her sixth child and third daughter.

17. The Mount Zion Church is north of the town of Fayetteville, to which
Chesnutt has now returned.

18. Rockfish Village, on Little Rockfish Creek, was just south of Fayetteville.
The then-new Hope Mills gave the town south of Fayetteville its current name.
The Republican party, heavily supported by black voters and committed to

August 12. Yesterday I went to town after school, and lost my watch chain on the way. I bought another and a key for a quarter dollar from my old friend "Cheap John." I went to Mr. Harrises, and practiced a little. Returning home, I met Democratic Delegation from Gray's Creek, for the Grand Democratic Rally last night. I suppose they had a "large-sized" time. I hear today that Buxton is elected; and Hyman, the colored candidate for Congress in the eastern part of the state [19] is also elected. This some what weakens the Democratic victory.

To-day I have been reading magazines, Algebra, Theory of T,[20] U.S. History and so on. This evening I went over to Leary's,[21] ate peaches, &c. and so on.

Aug. 14.   Lost in a swamp.

"Nathan," said my father to me after nooning-time, one day, "I want you to saddle the old gray mare, and go over to Tom Bright's after some seed-corn. Take a bag and get a bushel, in the ear." "You had better be spry or you'll not get back before night.

Tom Bright lived about five miles of[f], on the opposite side of a large swamp. The country on our side was very thinly settled at that time, but on the other side it was more thickly settled. We had made but a poor crop the year before. Farmer Bright was a celebrated farmer, and raised the best corn in the county.

---

blacks' participation in political life, had come to power in North Carolina in 1868 but by 1874 was already losing its brief dominance. It was swept from power in 1876.

19. Buxton is Joseph Potts Buxton (1826–1900), onetime antisecessionist candidate to the 1861 state convention, longtime supporter of Negro rights, and eventual Republican party leader. A Fayetteville lawyer, he was reelected as superior court judge in 1874. Hyman is John A. Hyman, a black Republican elected to the House of Representatives from the Second Congressional District (the so-called Black Second) in 1874. Hyman was not renominated and did not run in the election of 1876.

20. *Theory and Practice of Teaching: or, The Motives and Methods of Good Schoolkeeping,* by David Perkins Page, principal of the State Normal School of New York. Published in the mid-1840s, this volume was regularly reprinted as late as 1899.

21. The family of Chesnutt's near-contemporary John S. Leary, who became a lawyer in Fayetteville and was the second black admitted at the North Carolina bar.

I saddled the mare and started at once. In about two miles, I struck into the swamp. It was a large swamp about two miles wide and 10 miles long. After riding as I thought about two miles, I thought I ought to be getting out of it. But instead of getting out of it, I was getting deeper and deeper into it, as I soon found, to my dismay.

I did not know the roads any too well, and had taken a wrong turn. I tried to retrace my steps, but they were lost in grass, as the roads were but little used. As the weather was cloudy, I could not divine my way by the sun, and I knew not which way to go. I was lost in the swamp. I wandered on for several hours, through blind roads. Night was coming on, and the tall trees and thick underbrush made my road particularly gloomy and sombre. The frogs began to croak, and I heard the howl of wolf afar of[f] (there were a few left around that part of the country) and it sounded ominous indeed to me. What if the wolves should attack me? I had no weapon to defend myself. My horse was but a poor runner. They would overtake me, and devour me.

Filled with these gloomy reflections, I still continued my way. It had been cloudy all day, but now it began to clear off, and although the woods were so thick that I could not see it, the moon began to shine[.]

In a short time I heard the sound of falling water, and turning into a side road, soon arrived at an old deserted mill. Here the woods were somewhat closed out, and looking at the Pole-star, I found my course, and taking an old road in that direction a few miles ride brought me to a house. I stayed there during the night, and in the morning thanked the people, and inquired the way to Farmer Bright's, where I soon arrived. I related my adventure, got my corn, and one of the farmers boys carried me into the home-road, where I soon arrived, to the great relief of my parent, who didn't know what was become of me.———— Chas. Chesnutt

The above is my first real attempt at literature. The reader will please pardon all faults an[d] errors and I will try and do better next time. (If any one reads it besides myself).

Aug 15th. To-day I went to Mr. Harris', worked algebra, played on the organ, read and so forth. I got a "Barnes' History of the

47

U.S.[22] It is arranged in epochs, each containing the history of some particular time. Epoch 1 extends from 1492, when Columbus discovered America[,] to 1607, the settlement of Jamestown Virginia. It treats of the Spanish French and English explorations, discoveries and settlements on the continent.

Epoch 2. From 1607, the settlement of Jamestown, to 1775, the breaking out of the Revolutionary War. Its title is "The development of the colonies.

Epoch 3. The Revolutionary War. This epoch extend[s] from 1775 & the breaking out of the Revolutionary War to 1787, the adoption of the Constitution.

Epoch 4. The development of the States. This epoch extends from 1787, the adoption of the Constitution, to 1861, the breaking out of the Civil War, or Rebellion.

Epoch 5. The civil War. This epoch extends from 1861, the breaking out of the Rebellion, to 1865, Lee's surrender, and contains an account of that gigantic struggle.

Epoch 6. Reconstruction and passing Events. This epoch extends from the close of the civil war to the present time.

This is a brief one-term school history of "Our Country", but I like the arrangement of the topics, and, the whole book very well indeed. I may from time to time give an outline of some part of it from memory.

Aug. 17th. I received a letter from C. R. Harris the other day (14th) stating that he had engaged an assistant teacher, Miss Victoria Richardson,[23] a neice of his. Unless there is funds sufficient to employ another assistant, this knocks all my chance of getting back to Charlotte "higher than a kite." But in this case I can get a school in the country, and practice government better. I am advancing steadily in my studies. Yesterday (16) I went to Mr. H's, played on the organ, and then went up to the School-

22. Barnes is not the author but the publisher. A. S. Barnes and Company was the chief purveyor of the new literature produced for and about public schools in the wake of the 1840s common school movement. "Barnes' History" is *A Brief History of the United States for Schools,* by Joel Dorman Steele, published by A. S. Barnes in 1871 and reissued in 1874.

23. Victoria Richardson, from another black Cleveland family associated with education and the professions, continued to work with her uncle Cicero Richardson Harris and eventually became principal of the Preparatory Department at Livingstone College in Salisbury.

house and played a tune or so on that. It is a nice one, "Mason & Hamlin" 5 octave. I like it very much. I borrowed a chair from the school house yesterday to sit in at my school.

August 21st.   A Fight.

This evening Mr. Revels,[24] going home from his work, heard the bell of his cow, over about the back of Joe. Atkins's field, went back there after the cow, and began calling her. Joe Atkins was at home, and being "tight" he heard Mr. Revels and started over that way cursing him, and swearing he would kill him &c. Laura, his wife, and Bill, his son, started after him. Mr. Revels seeing him coming, raised his ax and stood on the defensive. Joe rushed up on him, tried to take the ax away from him, and threw him down, and got on top of him. Mr. Revels, not turning loose the ax[,] they had a tussle. Bill came up and tried to pull him off. Just then Laura came up and threw a brick at him, and, as I heard, smashed it to pieces over his head. The combined efforts of Bill and Laura got him off. I did not hear the rest of this affair, but I will conjecture it. Mr. Revels backed off a little, shook his fist, and threatened Joe largely, said he would have satisfaction, and scared Joe a little. At night Joe came down to Mr. Revels' to talk, to reason with him. But Mr. Revels would n't talk, so I don't know how they have, or will fix it. P.S. Mr. Revels got out a writ against Joe, and Joe submitted and paid the costs. Mr. Revels said "If it hadn't for that boy, 'Bill,' I expect he would have [illegible word: walloped?] me pretty Bad.

Another Incident. Yesterday Jack Pettifoot, lying asleep in the cooper shop where he works. A woman was in there joking with the men, and picked up a shaving and threw it on him. Jack jumped up, rushed out of the shop, down the hill, into the creek, and started down the stream into deep water. He fell several times, and when he got out of his depth Andy Murchison, a workman, got him out after he sank several times. When he returned to consciousness he was conveyed home. Charley went to see him last night and asked him, what was the matter. He said "nothing." Charley asked him why he was so mad[.] He said

24. Jonathan Revels is registered in the 1880 United States Census as a mulatto male, aged sixty, occupation "works on farm." By 1880 he was married to Ann Chesnutt, Charles Chesnutt's paternal grandmother. The census lists Joseph Atkins as a white male, aged forty-three, occupation "clerk in store."

"He and the boys were playing throwing water on each other and wet him". Charley said he had quite a wild look in his eyes. He has a very ungovernable temper, and this is very strange.

Aug 23rd. Yesterday I went up to Mr. Harris and stayed nearly all day. Played the organ, and read 1 vol "Uncle Tom's Cabin."[25] It was no ways old to me, although I have read it before.

Aug. 25. Today it has been very wet[,] muddy, disagreeable, and rainy. This morning it was pretty cool. It made me think of sending for my overcoat. I shall send for it if Mr. C. R. H.[26] does not employ me. He will leave Cleveland, God willing, Saturday, the 26 proximo. I have just finished Barnes U.S. History, and have nearly finished Pages Theory and Practice of Teaching. I think I shall now read, "A View of S.A. and Mexico," by a citizen of the U.S." an old, but doubtless a valuable book. I have reread Pickwick Papers,[27] by Dickens, and it was not at all old to me. I enjoyed it very much. It is a splendid book.

As I have been reading "Quackenbos' Composition & Rhetoric,"[28] I shall write some essay[s], anecdotes, &c. in this book. One is here given.

A Storm at sea.

The ship went forward at the rate of ten knots an hour, under full sail.

The captain stood on deck, near the helm. "Jim," said he to the helmsman, "do you think we will have fine weather all day?"

"Dunno, cap'n" said the old tar. "I don't like the looks of

25. Harriet Beecher Stowe's antislavery best-seller, for Chesnutt and his contemporaries the inevitable image of the novel as agent of social change, was published in 1852.

26. Cicero Harris.

27. *A View of South America and Mexico,* by John Milton Niles, was published in 1826. Dickens's *Pickwick Papers* was serialized in 1836–37 and printed in book form in 1837. For Page's *Theory and Practice of Teaching,* see 46.

28. *Advanced Course of Composition and Rhetoric . . . Adapted for Self-Instruction, and the Use of Schools and Colleges* (1854 and often reprinted), by George Payne Quackenbos, principal of the Collegiate School in New York. The subsequent piece of writing, while unremarkable in itself, shows Chesnutt's early habit of setting himself writing exercises inspired by school texts—a kind of self-inflicted homework—as an act of self-discipline.

that little cloud over on the larboard." "Besides there's a gale in these parts about this time every year." "Last year, when I was shipped on the Rover, a —"

"Never mind, Jim," said the captain, you can spin that yarn some other time". Giving a few commands to the mate, he went below.

In a few hours the little cloud noticed by Jim, had overspread the sky, and hidden the sun from our view. The wind died down; the vessel lay in a dead calm. An oppressive silence was on everything.

But this did not last long, in a few minutes the storm came on. Every thing on board was made snug and tight[.] The storm increased in its fury. The waves rolled mountains high. The thunder rumbled and rolled and seemed to strike the heavens; the lightnings darted their forked tongues across the sky in wild confusion. The rain fell in torrents. One moment the ship was poised high on the summit of some huge wave, and the next, it seemed almost swallowed up in the depth of waters.

In the wild turmoil of waters, the ship seemed as a child's toy in the hands of a giant.

It was a scene of indescribable grandeur; a scene well calculated to inspire feelings of terror.

The passengers tremblingly enquired of the captain whether there was much danger. He quieted their fears by assuring them there was none. The vessel was new and well made, and was manned by a splendid crew.

In a few hours the storm subsided; the sea grew less rough, and the clouds rolled away, and the rainbow, emblem of a divine promise, appeared.

The ship had sustained little or no damage in the encounter and in a short time was put in good trim, and proceeded on her way homeward.

Lines[29]
For those here below,
Who the good and the true
And the beautiful do love

29. The "Storm at Sea" essay was carried over from one left-hand page of the journal to the next left-hand page; this verse was written on the intervening page, possibly at a different time.

There is laid up a palm,
And a robe and a crown,
And a heavenly mansion above.

Our Saviour did come,
To offer a home,
To all who on him shall believe.
And if we will love him
And serve him below,
The reward we shall surely receive.

Let all of us strive,
While on earth we do live,
To serve our kind Father on high.
So that, when life is o'er,
And we dwell here no more,
He will call us to Him in the sky.

Bruno

Dear old Bruno! Though you are old and blind, yet you are loved by me!

Bruno is a large jet-black Newfoundland dog, and was, when he first came into my possession, a splendid specimen of the canine species.

He came into my possession in a somewhat curious manner. One wet rainy day when picking my way along the slippery pavement, I noticed an individual walking a short distance in front of me; he was staggering along as though he was slightly intoxicated, or "tight," a term expressive of a limited degree of that unnatural condition.

He was accompanied by a large Newfoundland dog, Bruno, who kept close to his side.

Having to stop at a place on some business, I lost sight of this individual for a short time; but when I reentered the street, I noticed a crowd gathering a short distance off. Hearing that an accident had happened, I hastened to the spot, and elbowing my way into the crowd, found the passenger before mentioned, lying half on the pavement, and half in the gutter, in a state of unconsciousness. His dog lay by him, whining dismally and snuffing at him and licking his face and hands.

As it is a noticeable fact that crowds are always willing to witness an accident, it is equally as noticeable that they are very slow to render any assistance in such cases, (except in case of a fire or something of the kind, when they manage to do about as much harm as good.[)] In this case the man had lain on the ground several minutes, and no one had stirred a finger to remove him.

I ordered him moved into a drugstore near by where by a plentiful application of the usual remedies, he was restored to consciousness[.]

I then had him removed to bed in a boarding house nearby, and examining his injury, I found it very dangerous indeed. Perscribing and ordering some physic (I am a physician), I departed on my rounds, promising to return in the evening.

Returning at the appointed time, I found my patient considerably worse than I supposed. He was far advanced in a consumption, and would not have lasted much longer; walking along the slippery street, he had been struck with a sudden pain and had slipped and fallen, and had sustained a severe internal injury. He was failing rapidly, and could last but a few hours.

He was an attache of a theatrical company which had exhibited at ———— a few days before, but on account of some misunderstanding, had remained behind.

His dog sat by the bed side, looking wistfully at his face, and licking the thin hand which hung down by the side of the bed. The sick man spoke: "I am a lone man, without money or friends, except my good Bruno. Poor Bruno! You have stuck to me through thick and thin. You have accompanied me in all my rambles, shared my fortunes and misfortunes. Doctor, I am going, but when I am gone take care of Bruno. He is a dog that few men would refuse to own."

I promised him that I would and asked if I should send for a clergyman. He answered in the affirmative, and I dispatched a servant for one: but the poor fellow soon after became delerious and expired before the preacher arrived.

I had the necessary funeral ceremonies attended to, and took the dog Bruno home with me. He soon got over his bereavement, he became the pet of the family[,] the playmate of the children, and devotedly attached to me. Though he is old and blind, yet he is the same, dear old Bruno.

C. W. C.

> When grim old Death on me doth call,
> To shuffle off this mortal coil,
>> May I prepared be, by God's grace,
> To meet my maker face to face.
>
>> And when before his throne I stand,
> May I be placed at His right hand,
>> And there with *Him* forever live
> Who *only*, happiness can give.
>
> Then with hosts of angels bright
>> Clad in dazzling robes of white
> I forever there shall stay,
>> In the bright eternal day.
>>   C. W. C.

Charlotte

Sept 7. I arrived safe here (at Charlotte) Sunday, the 4th ult. and carried my trunk to Elder Moore's,[30] and breakfasted there. Went to Mr. Schenck's[31] after breakfast to see Mr. H, and he had made arrangements for me to board there. I am now staying there. (here).

My school duties began Monday. Our school is very large. Have for another teacher Miss V. Richardson, neice of Mr. H. from Cleveland, O.

Jan. 9th 1875. We had a vacation of 2 weeks, beginning, Friday, Christmas Day. I spent the whole Christmas Holidays in preparing for an entertainment at the Templar's Hall[.] On Thursday after Christmas we played "The first Glass" a temperance Drama.[32] We had several songs and comic pieces. On thursday night the audience was small, but they were well pleased with the performance; and we would have had a large audience Friday night, but the ground was covered with sleet, and it was still falling. As it was, the Audience was smaller than Thurs-

30. Probably J. W. Moore, listed in *Beasley & Emerson's Charlotte Directory* (1875) as colored preacher of the Zion Methodist Church.
31. Possibly either William or Burt Schenck, both listed as mulatto males in the 1870 United States Census.
32. The play Chesnutt describes is *The First Glass; or, The Power of Woman's Influence* (1868), by Nellie H. Bradley, a prolific writer of temperance plays.

day night, and as it somewhat discouraged the actors, I do not think the performance was quite as good as Thursday night's, although the principal play, "the First Glass" was well acted both times.

The following is the cast of Characters and synopsis of Scenery and Play,

Played at Templar's Hall Dec 31st 74

Frank West a teetotaller	Mr. Geo Dillard
Alice West, a rigid tetotaler, and Frank's sister,	Mattie McCullough
Molly Mason a thoughtless young lady	Jennie Jones
Howard, a toper and gambler	Ed. Butler
Maggie & Bessie, Howard's Children	Geo Williams, & Sarah White
Servant	C. W. C.

Scene 1. *A Parlor.* Mollie Mason discovered reading . . . . . . Enter Alice & Frank West. They exchange greetings . . . . Enter servant with wine. Mollie offers wine to Alice, who refuses . . . . . . Offers it to Frank, who first refuses. She insists and in a playful manner commands him . . . . . He yields and drinks the wine . . . . Arises to go, and pulling out his handkerchief to wipe his lips, drops a paper . . . . Exit in . . usual form . . . . Mollie asks Alice why she is so sad. Alice tells her Frank's History and gives her a good temperance lecture: Molly is sorry that she induced Frank to drink. Exit Alice. Mollie reproaches herself, and affirms that she will devote herself to the Temperance cause.

Curtain.

Scene II. A year is supposed to have elapsed.

Frank West and Howard discovered sitting at table in a rough room, gambling.

Table covered with cards, bottles and glasses. Howard wins money, urges West to try again . . . . West has but $1.25 left, which belongs to his sister. . . . At last he yields . . . . Howard wins again . . . . West in despair . . . . West paces floor in agony . . . . Howard induces him to put up his watch, which he loses . . . . West admires watch . . . . Lays down across chairs and goes to sleep[.]

Enter Maggie and asks him to come home . . . . He rudely repulses her; she retires and leads in Bessie . . . . . . Maggie &

Bessie lead him from the room. During this time West has been leaning head on table . . . . Raises it and paces the floor in despair . . . . at last takes out pistol to shoot himself . . . . . . Enter Alice and Mollie grasping his arms . . . Glass and pistol fall to floor with a crash, pistol going off in the air . . . . They all kneel . . Solo—"In the dark and midnight stilly hour" . . . .

Curtain

Scene III. Parlor, same as first. Alice and Mollie seated.

Enter Maggie and Bessie . . . . Enter Howard and Frank, well dressed and reformed. Maggie and Bessie run to meet Howard, lead him to a seat and take places on each side of him . . . . Howard introduces Frank as President of Temperance Soci. Frank introduces Howard as Secretary . . . . Girls request them to be seated. Frank seats himself by Mollie, Howard by Alice . . . . Frank leads Mollie to front of stage and introduces her as his future wife . . . at the same time Howard leads Alice out and introduces her as his future wife. They shake hands across. Maggie and Bessie advance to front of stage with hands around each other . . . .

Alice and Mollie . . . . "None but teetotal Husbands for us".

Frank and Howard, "For us teetotal wives" Mag. & Bess. "And as the days pass merrily by"
How happy shall pass our lives."

Tableau, Maggie & Bessie cent. Arms around each other, Alice and Howard left, Frank and Mollie right, Gentlemen on the outside.

Curtain.

"All's *well that ends well.*"

. . . . .

On Thursday night next, the [no number supplied] of Jan, if the weather is good we will play "the abstinate Family", a farce in one act.

On night before last I went to the Opera House. "Clara [illegible name: Wildner's?] Troupe played "East Lynne, or the Earl's Daughter"[33] it was splendid. They finished up the

---

33. Popular first as a novel by Mrs. Henry Wood (1861), then as a long-running play by Clifton W. Tayleure (1867), *East Lynne* is the story of an aristocratic woman who runs off with another man, then disguises herself and returns in order to care for her children.

performance for the night with a "Glorious Farce." It was very laughable. I laughed till I was nearly sick. I want to revise it a little and re-act it next Thursday night, if I can.

March 20, 1875. [In Pittman shorthand:] It has been a long time since I wrote anything in this journal. Today I shall write a little. I have been studying phonography for a month or so, and write this in it. I have been studying German lately, and am near through my grammar. I like German very much. I am getting along finely with the girls. I heard last night that J. J. is back. I do not know whether to believe it or not. At any rate, I am going with her until I find that it is getting out, and then I will [illegible]. . . . I am going to Booths this evening and feel Joe's [illegible word: legs? hugs?] Just think! How fine the girls are! . . . Joe loves me, Emma loves me! And I like to have forgotten, Jane loves me. I guess that I am doing well [illegible words] a girl around. The civil rights bill has passed! Glorious! Hurrah for the 43rd Congress! They were a long time about it, but it has passed at last![34]

[Eight pages of only partially legible shorthand exercises follow.]

Apr. 6th 1875. Gestern sandte Ich fur ein Deutsches Worten Buch, und ein [illegible word] Robertus ein Werk auch das Geschwind Schreiben Kunst. Wann Sie kommen dann wird ich Deutsch und Kurz Hand studieren suchen. Ich glaube dass Ich wird lassen Josie allein fur ein Zeit. Gestern Abend Ich fragte wenn Sie brauchtete zum Temperance Zusammenfluss gehen, und Sie sagte, "Ja, aber nicht ohne Frau Richardson geht,["] als ob Sie was mir furchtend[.] Sie ist Narrisch. Dass ist was Ich sage.[35]

34. Jo or Josie, the object of Chesnutt's infatuation in his Charlotte years, is unidentified, as are the other girls he names. The Civil Rights Act of 1875 prohibited racial discrimination in public accommodations such as inns, hotels, and railways. A more radical provision extending this prohibition to schools was defeated before the bill was passed. The act's antidiscrimination provisions were largely voided by a Supreme Court ruling in 1883.
35. "Yesterday I sent for a German dictionary and a [illegible word] Robertus a work also the art of quick writing. When they come I will try to study German and shorthand. I think that I will leave Josie alone for a while. Yesterday

Letzen Nachte ging ich mit Josie, liebe Josie, dem Fraulein Viktoria, und dem Herrn Malord auf [illegible name: Lethells?] Haus woher wir spielten Karten lange.

Heute ging ich hinaus nach dem [illegible: Lethells?] Ich begegnete dem Professoren Nies, und redete mit ihm vor der Schule, der deutsche Sprache und anderen Dingen. Er lieh mir ein Buch, ein Lustspiel in funf Anzügen. Ich lass einige Seiten darauss, mit der Hilfe eines Deutsche Worterbuch des Herrn Nies. Ich ging [illegible word] meinem Buch, aber es war noch nicht angekommen. Ich höffe, dass es wird Morgen kommen.[36]

Apr. 26th 1875. Sonn Abend, letzend Sonnabend war mir solche ein Tag! Solche ein Zeit Ich hatte! Liebe Josie! Wie Ich liebe dich!

Du liebest mir, Ich weiss es wohl.

Ich bin solche ein Schurze, aber Ich liebe meine Josie.[37]

Mai 4th. Seit dem Ich habe den oben geschrieben, Ich habe Deutsch viel studiert. Jetz[t] lese ich die Zeitungen sehr wohl. Ich habe under den deutschen viel gesprochen. Und ich lese gerade Lustspiel, dem ich von dem Herrn Nies borgen. Er ist ein guter Mensch.

Ich brauche der Deutsche Sprache, machtig, vollkommen zu werden.[38]

---

evening I asked her if she needed to go to the temperance meeting, and she said 'Yes, but not unless Mrs Richardson goes,' as if she was afraid of me. She is foolish. That's what I say."

36. "Last night I went with Josie, dear Josie, Miss Victoria, and Mr. Malord to [illegible name: Lethells?] house where we played cards a long time. Today I went out to the [illegible: Lethells?]. I met Professor Nies and talked with him about school, the German language, and other things. He lent me a book, a comedy in five acts. I read several pages from it, with the help of Mr. Nies's German dictionary. I went [illegible word] my book, but it hadn't arrived yet. I hope that it will come tomorrow." A marginal note identifies the comedy as *Das Leben ist Hart,* or *Life Is Hard.*

37. "Last Saturday was to me such a day! Such a time I had! Dear Josie! How I love you! You love me, I know it well. I am such a rascal but I love my Josie."

38. "May 4th. Since I wrote the above, I have studied German a lot. Now I read the newspapers very well. I have spoken a lot among the Germans. And I am now reading a comedy that I borrowed from Mr. Nies. He is a good person. I need to become competent and perfect in the German language."

May 20th 1875. One hundred years ago to-day a meeting of the patriotic citizens of "Charlotte-town" Mecklenburg Co. N.C., held an indignation meeting on Independence Square, in that city, and passed resolutions concerning the Stamp act and other British Oppressions.

A number of resolutions were drawn up, making what is called the Mecklenburg Declaration of Independence.[39] Today is being celebrated, &c. &c.

June 7th 1875. It has been several weeks since I have written any, but suffice it to say, that the Centennial turned out well. There was a grand procession, speeches, barbecues &c. We have been rehearsing a good deal lately at school, for the exhibition.

—— Of late, "meine Josie" ist ein wenig schau [scheu] [ge]worden, but I know, am well assured that "sie liebt mich," as much as Ich "liebe" sie. Heute war I there and wanted very much sie zu küssen, aber Ich konnte nicht. Aber ich habe Vergnugen und Freude mit ihrer to be. I have many different and rambling thoughts von der Josie; zuweilen, ich denke sie liebt mich, zuweilen ich denke sie liebt mich nicht.

Aber es ist klar, sie liebt mich. Obschon sie ist nicht refiniert or very damisch, ich liebe sie.[40]

In the country

On Saturday last I went up to a church called Jonesville or Jonahsville, I don't know which. I had heard from Mr. Davidson that a school, and of course, a teacher was wanted at that place.

I went up on the Statesville road. The conductor charged fifty cents for ten miles, which is just double the fare on the other roads, but as it is a little one-ox Rail-Road, it has to charge high.

39. On May 20, 1775, in the wake of the battles of Lexington and Concord, a public meeting at Charlotte passed resolutions that "do hereby dissolve the political bonds which have connected us to the mother country and hereby absolve us from all allegiance to the British Crown."

40. "Of late, 'my Josie' has become a little shy, but I know, am well assured that 'she loves me,' as much as I 'love' her. Today I was there and wanted very much to kiss her, but I couldn't. But I have pleasure and joy with her to be. I have many different and rambling thoughts of Josie; sometimes, I think she loves me, sometimes I think she loves me not. But it is clear, she loves me. Although she is not refined or very ladylike, I love her."

I[t] rained hard during the ride, and hailed too, but it had slacked up when I got off. I inquired the way to Jonesville church, and by dint of stopping and inquiring at every house, and by climbing fences and crossing cotton fields, I arrived at Jonesville.

Where the "ville" was I am not able to say, for there was but one house within nearly a half mile of the "church". The church itself was a very dilapidated log structure, without a window; but there was no need of one, for the cracks between the logs furnished a plentiful supply. A part of a log and clay chimney.

The interior was rougher than the outside; ten or a dozen "slabs" with legs made of oak saplings. A awful looking pulpit on the side of the room, and a lamp without a chimney suspended to the joists by a string. The chimney had been made for a fireplace but I pity the deluded being who imagines that a fire would burn in it.

When I arrived there there were four men beside the presiding elder, Mr. Davidson. The official board had been summoned to attend Quarterly conference, but this was all who came.

As they were waiting, I was introduced and we commenced talking on the school subject. They first said "yes they wanted a school,["] and then began maligning the other teacher [who] had taught the school. They tore him all to pieces in a few minutes. They said he was partial, and didn't half do his duty; that he went away without paying his board and washing bills. But the main fault was this, they said: he had one scholar, a little yellow girl, eight years old whom he treated better than the other scholars. I suppose they were prejudiced against her because she was yellow, for they are the blackest colored people up there that I ever saw.

I went to see Mr. Ayler, one of the school committee. He lived about 2 miles from the church, and while on the way to his house, I was regaled with an abstract of his history. "He had come down here 'bout five year ago, an' he didnt own nuffin but a hoss and keart, and his little boys. But he was a good shoemaker, and what with farming and shoemaking together, he had bought land, and was now one of the 'best off' men in the neighborhood."

My guide also gave me the history of several other school-teachers.

We arrived at once at Mr. Ayler's, and I immediately discovered that he was a German, and began a conversation in that language.

He asked me my name, where I was educated, &c. He asked me what countryman was I, and when I told him I wanted a colored school he told me in Dutch,[41] which was unintelligible to my guide, that the white people wouldn't respect me if I taught a colored school. Said that the colored people ought to have colored, and the whites, white teachers. He even offered me the white public school which I respectfully declined. But the upshot of the matter was that there was not money enough for me, so I bade him good day, and he bade me "good-by," which is the country salutation at parting, and went home with my guide.

The family with whom I stopped consisted of the old man, "Sam," his wife, his wifes mother and his son John and his wife, Alex his youngest son, and 5 or six children. The old man was a tall old gray headed fellow, with a straight face, and a heavy gray beard. The young man was pretty ugly. His wife Hannah was a buxom young woman, handsome and not quite as black as the "ace of spades." The old lady was a pleasant, polite, and lively woman. She was about 5 feet high, a little bent[,] wore a cap, and spectacles.

I had a real good supper, much better than I expected, fried chicken, corn bread, biscuits, light-bread, milk, strawberry-pie, &c. The only fault I had to find was, that the pie was not quite sweet enough for me. After supper we had a talk concerning schools[,] schoolteachers and preachers. The old man said that "you preachers and teachers are too hard on us. You want us to pay you thirty or forty dollars a month for sitting in the shade, and that is as much as we can make in 2 or 3 months." I tried to convince him that we earned it, but he couldn't see the point. He said "here's Uncle Edmund comes up here and wants us to give him five or six dollars and that's nearly 2 weeks wages.["]

I then asked how many times Mr. Davidson comes up there a year; they said "well, about twice." "How many members have you?["] "About fifty." "Well, I think it's a bad chance if you can't afford to give your elder ten cents apiece twice a year!"

41. Here as elsewhere Chesnutt uses "Dutch" for "Deutsch," or German.

"Well, but we haven't got any chance. We all of [us] work on other people's, white people's, land, and sometimes get cheated out of all we make; we can't get the money."

"Well, you certainly make something?" "Yes." "Now, I'll tell you. You say you are all renters, and get cheated out of your labor, why dont you send your children to school, and qualify them to look out for themselves, to own property, to figure and think about what they are doing, so that they may do better than you?"

"We can't do it," was all I could get out of them.

I learn from Mr. Davidson and from what I have seen myself, that they are a very trifling shiftless set of people up there, and their children are following in their footsteps.

Alex, my "guide", got down his note-book, and sang some tunes from it. He knew shape-notes, or square notes as they call them.

After that a hymn was given out, "Hark from the tomb," and sung through, after which the old gent gave us an "awful" long prayer during which I beleive I had a right good little nap. At any rate, I was dozing all the time.

I then retired to my chamber and slept all night on a feather bed (in June). The main room of the house contained four beds, all on one side of the room, and I had apprehended that I should have to occupy one, but I slept with Alex in a little shed room.

The next morning, Sunday, I got up, not as early as I had intended, but in time to prepare for breakfast, which was supper over again, only the chicken was "fixed" in two different ways.

After breakfast I was cleaning my shoes out in the yard, which the old lady observing, remarked that I "couldn't fault the country people," and I right from town cleaning my shoes on Sunday. I told her I couldn't do it on Saturday, for I wasn't there. She asked me why I didn't clean them on Saturday night and I answered that "I was too tired." I told her that I had been living with a preacher, as true a Christian as there is, and that he cleaned his boots on Sunday. The old lady did not exonerate me on this ground, but she hoped the Lord would forgive me.

When it was time to go to church I bid the old lady "good-by." She shook hands with me, and with a "God bless you" from her lips and I have no doubt from her heart I set out for church.

I had intended to describe the preacher and congregation at the meeting, the sermon, and to go into particulars, but suffice it to say that I staid till I had gotten dinner, and then in company with "Uncle Ed" set out for town, at which we arrived after a ten-mile walk. We took our time and so I was not fatigued and would have gone to church that night had it not rained.

June 14th. Reading over old dutch and shorthand pieces makes me feel somehow or other. Ich liebe dich Josie, Ich liebe dich! Ich weiss nicht, ob du liebst mich oder nicht. Aber, Gott weiss es, ich liebe dich. Ich bin nach Begier fur dich zerruckt gewesen, allein I erröthe das I kaum weg von dir bleiben. Weil man ein Mädchen liebt ist es nicht nothig ihn Narr zu machen. Du bist ein hässliches Mädel Aber die Liebe verbirgt viele, ja, alle Fehler.

Ich will dich zeigen dass Ich bin nicht ganz verruckt, and will not be so begierig nach dich.

Dessenumgeachtet, alles zum gegen, Ich liebe dich.[42]

The Breakfast Bell

There goes that bell. Some one, I'm told,
Has called it "tocsin of the soul"
'Tis false! Base Harrower of my peace,
When will thine everlasting ringing cease?
2.
An hour before I wish to rise,
    Before I've scarcely closed my eyes,
My very diligent Landlady,
    Is up and has her breakfast ready
And rings that bell with noise like thunder,
    To wake me from my peaceful slumber.
3.
And if I'm not down in a trice
She rings the old brass Humbug twice,

---

42. "I love you, Josie, I love you! I don't know whether you love me or not. But God knows, I love you. From desire I have been crazy for you, but I blush that I can hardly stay away from you. That a man loves a girl does not necessarily make him a fool. You are an ugly girl. But love hides a lot, yes, all faults. I will show you that I am not entirely crazy, and will not be so desirous for you. Notwithstanding, in spite of everything, I love you."

Comes up the stairs, comes to my door,
And rings an hour or less, or more.

4.

And when at last in deep despair,
I stick my fingers in my ears,
And yell out "I am coming"
She goes and leaves me there in peace,
And both my ears a-humming.

5.

But when at last I've washed and dressed,
Though still by sleepiness oppressed,
Down stairs in haste I go,
Expecting something at the least
   My sense of smell or taste to please.

6.

I find a great big dish of grits,
So cold 'twould give a Russian fits,
   Or toothache for a day to eat it,
   A plate of hash, some other trash,
A cup of muddy coffee to complete it.

7.

The man that calls that breakfast bell
The "tocsin of his soul,["]
The kind of soul that man has got,
Had better not be told.

C. W. Chesnutt

"Gute nacht, liebes Madel, und gluckliche Traume, von mir." [43]

June 16th. Beschenken, to reword, Ich erhielt gestern ein Buch nach dem ich schickte vor [blot] Woche. Es heiss: "Das Geschlechtliche System und seine Unordnungen." The grosste Theil lauft wegen Venery and Onanasm, wirklich eine schlechte Gewohnheit. Und wenn der liebe Gott will mich hilfen und halte in meinen guter Absicht, ich werde mich davon brechen. Gott zum Hilfe! [44]

43. "Good night, dear girl, and happy dreams, about me."
44. "Given, to reword, I received yesterday a book for which I sent [blot] weeks ago. It is called 'The Sexual System and its Disorders.' The largest part is about venery and masturbation, really a bad habit. And if the dear Lord will help me and keep me in my good intentions I will break myself of it. God help me!"

I received today a letter from Frank Hayman. He was well &c. He sent his respects und einem "Blatt, Rosenblatt" darin senden Josie. Schlimmer Schlemm![45]

July 1st 1875. Was examined to-day got first grade. I am going to Spartanburg tomorrow morning. Hope I shall be successful.

To J——.

1.

Farewell dear girl I leave you
I know not for how long.
But be it days or weeks or years
Your love shall ever be my song.

2.

It may be months ere I return,
It may be years for all we know,
But though we never meet again
I think of you where'er I go.

3.

We've passed full many a pleasant hour,
In each other's company,
And many of those pleasant hours
Were happy ones, to me.

4.

And now, my darling you must write
Assure me that you don't forget me.
And I shall, surely, write to you,
(That is if you will let me)
(Of course you will)

5.

And when ere long we meet again
I'll happy be, to find
I'll not have, as the proverb say,
When "out of sight" been out of mind.

6.

I very much, indeed would like
Another happy day to pass,
Like to the one I spent with you
On Sunday before last.

---

45. "and a 'Petal, Rose-petal' sent with it to Josie. Lousy scoundrel!"

7.

But as I cannot, I can say,
My blessing with you go,
And may you ever happy be,
My darling, darling Jo.

Erleuchten,	to	illuminate
Erzahlen	"	relate
Erleben	"	experience
Erdulden	"	endure
sich entrusten	to	become angry

"O wad some power the giftie gie us
To see oursel's as others see us,
It would frae mony a blunder free us
And foolish notion.

Burns[46]

Spartanburg, S.C. July 3rd 1875.

———I left Charlotte yesterday on the frieght-train, which carries an "accommodation coach".

The accommodation was wretched. The car was old and dirty, and full of dust. The cinders flew in the windows, and in all it was pretty disagreeable.

I took notice of some of the passengers, as follows.

There was one couple which attracted me particularly, a ladie and gentleman. I took them for a young couple in their honeymoon[.] The little looks and smiles, the gentle touches, and all the outward signs which mark the influence of the "tender passion[.]"

They were both handsome, spoke and looked like educated and refined people. I sat and envied them thier happiness.

There was another family. The father very portly, the mother also corpulent, and rather far advanced in a "delicate condition." Three fat curly headed children. This was a country family, doubtless. The animal faculties were very well developed in both. I noticed—but I forgot!

46. From Burns's poem "To a Louse, On Seeing one on a Lady's Bonnet at Church."

There was a lady on board. She was faded and wrinkled[,] highly painted, wore false teeth and was very talkative. She had a little girl along who was very precocious, and was always uttering some pert but seldom smart remark. The lady, I have since learned[,] is "Miss Belle Boyd, the confederate spy."[47] The little girl was "Miss Elmo Boyd[.]" The lady lectures, and the little girl recites verses of "original poetry."

I arrived at Spartanburg at about 4 o'clock, and sought out Mr. Lewis' Boarding place.

An old colored man is the landlord. The accommodation is moderate, and the terms are one dollar a day for "transient boarders[.]"

Spartanburg is a pleasant old place. It is up toward the mountains, and cooler than Charlotte. The place has two Rail Roads, The air Line,[48] and one to Columbia and Union.

I have seen but few homely people here.

Nearly every body is handsome especially the more refined.

There is a great deal of riding and the livery stable[s] have some very fine stock, and some splendid equipages. There are also some mineral springs here which I intend to visit.

I am going to teach about 10 miles from here in the country. My examination was begun today. It is entirely written and the questions are printed. I finished grammar today, and shall continue Tuesday. I am trying for "first Grade." Lewis got it.

It is pleasant here of evenings.

It is not good to be too religious or too modest and virtuous. Too much religion is fanaticism, and too much virtue prudery, which is nearly as disagreeable as immodesty.

Chas. W. Chesnutt
Spartanburg, S.C.

July 5th. Yesterday was the fourth of July, the 99 anniversary of American Independence. I suppose the Temperance Meeting proposed by Malord was held. Yesterday I went to the "Springs,"

47. Belle Boyd Hardinge (1843–1900), whose work as a Confederate spy contributed to Union defeats in the Shenandoah valley, told her story in *Belle Boyd in Camp and Prison* (1865).

48. The second railroad through Spartanburg was the Danville line.

and today also. They are very pleasantly situated at the foot of a hill, and the grounds are relieved by rustic seats and Bowers.

There is a small fountain which is supplied from the hillside, and plays continually. There is a stand where refreshment[s] are kept, ice cream, lemonade[.][49]

In the country, July 10th 1875.   I am in the woods again. I came up here yesterday afternoon. I am in a large old frame house. My room is upstairs. It is spacious and tolerably pleasant. The people are very anxious to please. I have not been anywhere away from where I now am.

I begin to feel a little Charlotte-sick, and to wish I could see [name blotted]. If she were here I would be contented. I wonder if she will be true to me? I love her, and she has loved me. Will she continue to do so? I have written to her and should probably get an answer if I were at Spartanburg, and now I don't think I shall go there till next Saturday. I wish I could write to her without her mother's reading the letters. I would write nothing improper, of course, but I would pour out my heart. It is a shame for a fellow to be obliged to confine himself to such cold sentences as a mother will hold discreet.

I love the girl, and I hope she loves me and will continue to do so. Here is a lock of her hair! I kiss the lock of hair and press it to [my] bosom[.] Would it were she!

As much as I have striven—I love her, and if I shall continue to possess her love, I never will, God help me, act in any way but that in which every gentleman should act toward a lady. God knows I love her.

———— I wish I were about twenty-five years old and had about a thousand dollars or so, and she were a few years older, I'd marry her, if she'd have me and I think she would.

———— But I shall strive to be contented, and happy, if I can be. Nothing would make me so happy as her presence.

It is a strange thing—a little strange why women have so much influence with men. They are the "weaker vessel," yet they often wield the stronger. I love a girl who is not strictly speaking,

49. Of the several springs in the neighborhood of Spartanburg, Chesnutt probably refers to Beach Springs, eight or ten miles to the west.

any ways good-looking. To me, all her faults are nothing. I love her, and as "charity covereth a multitude of sins," love hides all defects. I would give anything for her photograph,——Pshaw! What a fool I am, sitting here [blotted word] I thought I was more of a man than that.

> "And O, my Eppie
> My jewel my Eppie,
> Wha wadna' be happy
> Wi' Eppie Adair?
> By love and by beauty,
> By law and by duty,
> I swear to be true to
> My Eppie Adair.

> "And O, my Eppie,
> My jewel, my Eppie,
> Wha wadna' be happy,
> Wi' Eppie Adair?
> All pleasure exile me,
> Dishonor defile me
> If e'er I beguile thee
> My Eppie Adair!!"[50]

"Mein Leben, Ich liebe dich."[51]

July 12th. I have made up my mind to try and do right, and to get religion if I can. Lord, help me to pray and to seek thy love. Lord, give me thy grace, and make a man, a Christian of me. I never have been happy since I quit that first attempt I made to seek the Lord. Even at times when I was as happy as I could be in sin, then I felt I was doing wrong, was condemned by my own mind. I can and do give up such things as are not compatible with the life of a Christian. Here in these wilds I have no temptations, or but few, and God will enable me to overcome those. Were I in Charlotte I would have no temptations that I could not resist, when helped by God. "Religion never was designed to make our pleasures less". I believe it, if there is any pleasure, any true pleasure [it is] in religion for I have

50. Again from a poem by Robert Burns, Chesnutt's favorite poet at this stage.
51. "My life, I love you."

69

tasted the apple of sin and though it was sweet to the tongue, there was a worm gnawing at the core which gave it a bitter taste. I never did a mean action and went to bed without feeling condemned. I prayed to God once—well he has answered my prayer so far. May he continue to answer the same. May he bless me with his grace [and] let me serve him. I want to feel like a man and a Christian, to walk the earth with a firm step, and to feel that I am honest. May God bless and protect me, and may he bless and protect *her* who is dear to me. Guard her from sin's advances. Keep her virtuous and pure!———

Today I am to begin my school. Schools are certainly needed here. The people are deplorably ignorant. The man I board with doesn't know the Lord's prayer, perfect. He says "Give us this day————as we forgive those who trespass against us." It is a great pity.

July 13. Yesterday I began my school. I had 26 scholars, but some "can't come no more right now, till we finish layin' by". Nearly all were girls. One is another Mary Young, in looks. I got scared as soon as I saw her come in. But she has not, and I hope will not, give me any trouble. Her mouth and eyes are almost precisely like Mary Young's and though I think I can manage her, yet when she glares on an offending little boy, she looks about as much like a tiger as Mary can. I shall try and treat her kindly as I can. I don't intend to punish (ferule) any if possible. I was awful lonesome yesterday afternoon. Could think of nothing but Charlotte and Josie. I want to go to Spartanburg, and get my mail. There is sure to be a letter from Jo, if she is in Charlotte. But I must wait till Saturday.

> "God bless you Jo"
> "Would my Josephine know if I love
>   let her take
> My last thought at night and my first when I
>   wake,
> When my prayers and best wishes
>   preferred for her sake."
>   —Cowper

Afternoon—School was small today. My "Mary Young" wasn't there. It is a tiresome business, teaching three classes, all as dull as can be. Over half my scholars [are] in the alphabet. I tried singing this morning. They said they knew "Shall we gather &c." and I sang it. The larger girls "Miss Louisa Peak" &c. whined it through their noses in a decidedly droll manner. All the scholars say "dō," "thē," "ā," "ăre," &c. which I must first "unteach" them (if I may coin a word.[)] I shall try and do the best I can, for it is my duty, and besides, if I get paid for it at all, I shall get well paid. I have not seen the trustee yet, but shall try and see him this week. I think I am improving in health already. I am trying to be cheerful.

I must now to my Latin lesson——There is an old history downstairs, published in 1793 or 4. The s's are all like f's in the old style.

I can see the mountains very plainly on my way to school, can distinguish the fields about on them.

July 14th. I have done very well to-day. I am not so lonesome, and, as a matter of course more contented. My school is small, only 21 today. I have been reading Byron and Cowper to-day. Cowper I like, but it requires a little work to follow him sometimes. Byron I like. "Don Juan" is rather unchaste. The language is none too pure, and the sentiments are decidedly impure.[52]

July 15th. I went to a prayer meeting last night, and did not get home until 12 o'clock. I then took a good bath and went to bed. At the prayer meeting we made arrangements about boarding[.] The following agreed to assist in paying Mr. Bomar $7.00 per. month:

Henry Moss	Gadson Gandel
Spencer Snoddie	Nelson Peak
Jerry Golikely	Adam Matthews
A. B. Goforth	Wade Fowler
Eliph. Golikely	Young Moore
Thos. Bomar	Samuel Peak

52. The romantic poet George Gordon, Lord Byron (1788–1824), was the archetypical libertine in the nineteenth century. William Cowper (1731–1800) was the author of the rustic-domestic minor epic *The Task*. See p. 44 for Chesnutt's copyings from Byron's *Don Juan*, whose first canto is the one he considers "unchaste."

Ned Williams   Joe Golikely
Jas. Huggins
Henry Canady

The prayer meeting was largely attended. There were more
women than men, and some of them had to come 3 or 4 miles.
They sing a great many of the "little spirituals." One I have
heard before in Spartanburg. The chorus has this in it, "O bear
me away on your snowy wing, to my eternal home." It is real
pretty, and I like it.

July 16th. I had about 20 scholars today. This is Friday, and one
week of my stay is past! It seems short. The first two or three
days I was here, I was "awful" lonesome, but now I have got to
liking the place, and the people very well. Life here is simple
and pleasant. I rise at six, read till breakfast, if it is not ready;
eat, read till school time, ½ past eight. Go to school[,] let out
at about three o'clock[,] come home and read till dark[.] Then
I can sit and sing, and recite pieces I have learned, think over
what I have read. I intend to read very little or none at night,
"for mine eyes' sake," and in order that I may sleep enough.—
This evening I went with Louis to get a load of oats, and had
a jolly ride over the stones, and up and down the hills. — I've
been reading Byron and Cowper to-day. Cowper's "Task" is
splendid. I will build a castle in the air. Cowper gives me the
materials in his Task. I don't wish my castle to be realized when
I am old and worn-out, but I would delight to lead a life like
the one he describes in "The Garden":

> "Domestic happiness, thou only bliss
> Of Paradise which has survived the fall"
> Though few now taste thee unimpaired and pure
> Or tasting long enjoy thee! too infirm
> Or too incautious to preserve thy sweets
> Unmixed with drops of bitter, which neglect
> Or temper sheds within the crystal cup,
> Thou art the nurse of Virtue, in thine arms,
> She smiles, appearing, as in truth she is
> Heaven-born and destined to the skies again," &c. &c.[53]

53. From Cowper's *The Task*, book 3: "The Garden," lines 41–50.

I would wish my life to be like that. Rural retirement[,] plenty to occupy the mind and hands. A dear companion to share my joys. A happy family growing up around me, and when having had enough of the world, I pass away to a better "My children shall rise and call me blessed" and I be regretted and remembered with love and respect by all who knew me.

This is enjoying life! I believe that life was given to us to enjoy, and if God will help me, I intend to enjoy mine.

And I hope I shall endeavor to be truly happy in life and glorious in death.

July 17th. I got up soon this morning, and went to Spartanburg. I didn't get a letter from Jo nor anyone else. I got my certificate from Richardson. It was a "splendid" First Grade. I saw Mr. and Mrs. Daniel, wrote four letters & cards. A letter to Miss Richardson, one to Mr. Harris, one to Mrs. Schenck and a card to the P.M. at Charlotte, requesting him to forward all mail for me at Charlotte, to Spartanburg. I saw in town, Mr. Maxwell, Scott, both were doing very well indeed. We started home about an hour by sun and got here after ten o'clock. I then ate supper, which I should not have done. I am writing this at nearly eleven. I don't think I'll write again at eleven soon.

July 19th 1875. Yesterday was Sunday. Having been to town the day before, yesterday morning I was a little lowspirited[,] besides I didn't sleep well Saturday night. — I went to Sunday school late, but the school had decamped to Shady Grove meeting-house, and thither we continued our way and arrived[.] It was three miles from here the way we went. I heard a tolerably good sermon from the first preacher, but I got some new scripture expositions from the latter preacher. He said: Explaining the Dives and Lazarus parable.[54]

Dives didn't want his brethren to come to hell. He knew that the more there were there the hotter the fire would be; he quoted a proverb in this wise: "The more fat on the fire the hotter it burns," thus giving Dives request a very selfish motive. — Several others I can't think of them now[.] Came home to dinner about four o'clock. It was "awful" hot yesterday. In the

54. See Luke 19.

evening I got Mr. Bomar's mule and rode over to Mr. Turners (3 miles)[,] the school trustee, to find out concerning my school. He said the school would probably run but 2 months, and that as it was a second grade school, I could not get first grade pay. I asked him would I then get only second? He said he would consider my certificate as favorably as possible, and I'll probably get about $40.

Only seven weeks more!

Hurrah   !   !   !   !   !   ! ! ! ! ! !

I guess I'll study for a Doctor. I must work, save money, study as hard as I can, till I'm ready, pocket and mind to enter a Med. Coll., and go to read in some Doc's Office. May I have success. God aid me and protect me. Herzlich.[55]

July 20th. I had twenty-three scholars to-day, three more than yesterday. They are progressing finely. The "Alphabet" know nearly all the letters, except one or two dull ones, Charley Bomar among them.

The girls in my A class can add and subtract, and one can multiply real well.

—One of the girls, my "Mary Young,["] got me to read a love-letter for her to-day. It was a proposal of marriage from a young Spartanburg chap, and nearly all of it was copied *verbatim et literatim* from a letter-writer. It ended up with several verses from popular songs, one of which was "Silver Threads among the Gold" viz.

> "Darling I am growing old,
> Silver threads among the gold,
> Shine upon my brow to-day,
> Life is fading fast away,
> But my darling you shall be,
> Ever young and dear to me,
> Yes my darling you shall be
> Ever young and dear to me"

——It is pretty and very popular. ——Another letter had all the following and several others. "The rose is red &c." ["]The world is round." My pen is poor &c.

---

55. "Sincerely."

My ride day before yesterday gave me a pain in my left side, and by sleeping without cover Saturday night and getting saturated with perspiration Sunday, and sitting in a draft and getting suddenly cooled, I am not as well as I might be, but considerably better than I was yesterday —— This afternoon I plowed some, cut some wood, brought some water, went to milking; all this is good for the health, besides if I go home, I don't want to be a raw hand.

Wird jemand das lesen, oder nicht? Wenn ich gehe zu Hause ich werde es dem Ludwig zeigen vermuthlich.[56]

> "Man's inhumanity to man
> Makes countless thousands mourn"
> > *Burns*

> "Variety's the spice of life."
> > *Cowper*

"The accusing angel flew up to heaven with the oath, and the recording angel, as he wrote it down, dropped a tear on the word, and blotted it out forever."
> > *Sterne's story of Lefevre*

> Auld Lang Syne.
> "Should Auld acquaintance be forgot
> And never brought to mind
> Should auld acquaintance be forgot
> > And days of auld lang syne.
> > Cho. For auld lang syne, my dear,
> > For auld lang syne,
> > We'll tak a cup o' kindness yet,
> > For auld lang syne.
> 2.   We twa hae run about the braes,
> > And pu'd the gowans fine,
> > But we've wander'd mony a weary foot
> > > Sin' auld lang syne.
> 3.   We then hae paidl't in the burn,
> > Frae mornin' sun till dine,
> > But seas between us braid hae roar'd

56. "Will anyone read this, or not? When I go home I will show it to Lewis, probably."

> Sin' auld lang syne.

4. And here's a hand, my trusty fine,
        Ane gie's a hand o' thine,
        And we'll tak a right guid willie-waught
            For auld lang syne.

5. And surely you'll be your pint-stoup
        And surely I'll be mine,
        And we'll take a cup o' kindness yet
            For auld lang syne.

Burns

"Miss Lexy, give us "Auld lang syne,' "my dear' ". Won't you?

> "The ugliest gal in this 'ere land,
>   Is that 'ere Louisa Peak."

———————

July 22nd. Didn't write yesterday.

Yesterday afternoon I came home[,] studied awhile, and then went out and plowed about an hour. I've been away from home, you may say, two years, and I think if nothing happens to prevent it, when I am through with this school, that I shall go home. I would like to work on the farm awhile. I can get employment up here, but I want to see the folks.

I guess they'll consider me a 'reprobate' and a 'renegade' for not sending any money home. But when a fellow does the best he can, why he can't do any better.[57]

Chesnutt

I guess Miss Vic is having a splendid time with her Johnny, her "jo." I guess Mr. Harris has gone to Fayetteville. I "puir bodie" am down here in this much abused negro-ruled state— South Carolina—Macedonia (that's the name of my schoolhouse) Beach Springs, (name of township,) School district no 2[.]

57. Chesnutt's father had looked to him for help supporting the family since he was fourteen, and he had gone to teach in Charlotte with the understanding that he would send money home. Andrew Chesnutt had failed as a storekeeper and taken up farming in 1874. Remarried after his first wife's death in 1871, he had a growing new family in addition to the six children from his first marriage.

July 28th. Hallo! Journal, How's your cromabomalopabus today? I haven't seen you in a coon's age. Haven't written anything in you since last Thursday. That's a week. —————— Last Friday a high-headed young gentleman of considerable color accosted me by the venerable title of "Uncle Chess." I, in a most graceful and polite manner informed him that I was unaware of sustaining that relationship to him, so he dropped down to Mr. Chess. — Saturday in the afternoon, I went over to Bowens Mill and took a swim—

Sunday I went to "Big Meetin'" at Wesleys Chapel and heard several harangues, a good many spirituals, came home and went to bed. Big Meetin' lasted till Monday night. Monday I had a big school, Tuesday a bigger, yesterday I had 43 scholars, which is about as many as I care to have. Yesterday and day before I have been basket-making[.] My old basket is pretty well on the way to completion!

Friday July 29th. Today will be the last day of the 3rd week of my school. I wish 'twas the last day of the 8th week— Yesterday Lewis went to town for me, and didn't get a letter. And I have written Pa one, Lewis one, Mr. Harris, Mis Vic.[,] Mrs. Schenck &c, and not one has written to me. Well! if nobody don't write to me I guess I can get along without.

> "I'll be merry and free,
> I'll be sad for naebody,
> If naebody care for me
> *I'll* care for naebody."
> —*Burns*

I think my "daddy" might write and tell me how they are getting along. But I suppose I am considered, as a prodigal, a reprobate, a spendthrift and everything else evil. But I cannot help it. I'll try and send my dad just as much money as I can, and just as many good words. I'll confess he has some good little cause to be displeased with me, for seventeen dollars a mo. sounds pretty big. But I will explain all to him, and may the Lord soften his heart!

July 30th 1875. Yesterday afternoon I began a willow basket. I guess they are pretty hard to make. This morning I went to see the threshers at Mr. Bushes. Then I went to the pond, where I staid in swimming a long time. I then came home, ate some "wasser-melon", and now I am going 8 miles with Ludwig after some trunks & I shall see the mountains plainly.

Afternoon July 31st—Saturday. About twelve o'clock Lewis and I set out for Colonel Colemans, or Capt. Coleman's for trunks. At Windmill Hill, about 5 miles from here we had a fine view of the mountains. I intend to go to them if possible, Saturday after next.

Twice to-day, or oftener I have been taken for "white." At the pond this morning one fellow said "he'd be damned" if there was any nigger blood in me. At Colemans I passed. On the road, an old chap, seeing the trunk, took me for a student coming from school. I believe I'll leave here and pass anyhow, for I am as white as any of them. One old fellow said to-day, "Look here Tom, here's a black fellow as white as you air".

Aug 7th 1875. To-day has been a happy day for me, for I was at last enabled to send pa some money. I sent him fifteen dollars to day. I sent Lewis two.[58]

Mr. Turner gave me \$37 and Richardson said that was a pretty good salary for a 3rd grade school. Ich stimmte ihm bei.[59]

I had a stormy time at meeting wednesday night but it's all right now.

Aug 11th 1875. Last Saturday I walked to spartanburg and ate heartily there, and then, contrary to the laws of nature and of health, set out immediately for home. I suppose that my food was not well digested. I sweated a great deal, and the wind blew very hard, and stopped the perspiration. I also got wet a little — This combination of forces formed a resultant of Bowel and lung sickness. My bowels hardly ever feel well. Night before last I took a dose of castor oil, and it "worked" me. But my stomach doesn't feel right yet. I hope and pray that I won't be dyspeptic or consumptive.

Teaching school in the country is pretty rough for those

58. This Lewis is Chesnutt's brother.
59. "I agreed with him."

who are not used to it. They don't know how to regulate their actions etc.

I began by taking exercise too much, and eating to[o] much, and it is about to injure me. "All ye Country Scholteachers take care of your health."

Today is Thursday. tomorrow is the last day of the week. Time "skedaddles[.]" Go ahead, old Time, but don't go too fast. I think *I'll* go home after this school is completed, "if I live and nothing happens."

"Honor thy father and thy mother, that thy days may be long in the land which the Lord thy God giveth thee—"   —Bible

Friday, Aug 13th 1875. I feel considerably better than I have been feeling for some days. I hope I shall be well in a few days, but I cannot shut my eyes to the fact that schoolteaching directly or indirectly, has ruined my health. I don't feel at all like a boy of seventeen should.

— Five weeks of school. Today closes my fifth week, and it is either, one-half, or five-eighths of my school term, and I don't care much which. This week has passed very well. I have made "tremendous" progress in algebra, almost finished Nat. Phil. Read "Universal Education",[60] and think it splendid, abounding in plain representations of undisputed facts, and clear demonstrations of excellent theories, many of which have been confirmed by experiment.

The following story is told in illustration of the incompetency of teachers:

"There is a story of a German schoolmaster, which shows the low notions that may be entertained of education. Stouber, the predecessor of Oberlin, the pastor of Waldbach, on his arrival at the place, desired to be shown to the principal school-house. He was conducted into a miserable cottage, where a number of children were crowded together without any occupation. He inquired for the master. "There he is," said one, as soon as silence could be obtained, pointing to a withered old man, who lay

60. *The Means and Ends of Universal Education,* by Ira Mayhew, superintendent of public instruction of the state of Michigan, was published in 1850 and often reprinted.

on a little bed in one corner. "Are you the master, my friend," said Stouber. "Yes, sir." "And what do you teach the children?" "Nothing, sir" ["]Nothing! how is that?" "Because," replied the old man, "I know nothing myself." "Why then were you appointed the school-master?" "Why, sir, I had been taking care of the Waldbach pigs a number of years, and when I got too old and infirm for that employment they sent me here to take care of the children."["][61]

When I finish that Elementary Algebra, I think I shall get a University Algebra and try for a "Peck's Mechanics[.]" I would like to get a "Bryant and Strattons Book keeping," but books cost a great deal of money. I think when I finish my Algebra, I shall take up Latin Grammar again, for if I have the remotest Idea of studying Medicine, a knowledge of Latin is very essential. When I received my salary, I bought Dickens "Barnaby Rudge". It is splendid. In it I found "Dolly Varden," after which character I suppose the Dolly Varden dresses, calico, were named. Sweet Dolly! Dear Emma! Faithful Joe! Honest Gabriel! Queer old Grip! Poor Barnaby! the Villain Rudge, the longsuffering Mrs. Rudge, the stupid old Joe, Chester, Edward, Hugh, Dennis the hangman, the amorous but ugly Nigel, the aspiring Tappertit, &c &c too numerous to mention, are all powerfully drawn and exhibit the authors versatility and scope of genius.[62] I wish I could write like Dickens, but alas! I can't. — Since my watch was fixed I get along a great deal better than I did before. A clock or watch is a necessary appendage to a school.

No one need tell me, that a school cannot be governed without the administration of corporal punishment, unless it is a very bad school indeed.

I have taught five weeks without it, and can very probably teach five more; at any rate, I shall *try*. — I have had an enrollment, for the month, of but 38, but a good many more will probably come. I want as large an enrollment, and as good

---

61. Taken from the section of *The Means and Ends of Universal Education* entitled "Well-Qualified Teachers Should Be Employed."

62. Chesnutt alludes to *Elements of Mechanics* (1866), by William Guy Peck, and *Bryant and Stratton's Common School Bookkeeping* (1861), by H. B. Bryant and H. D. Stratton. Dickens's *Barnaby Rudge* was published in 1841.

an average as possible. — The "committee" said they were going around to see about my board this week, but they "haint" gone yet.

I dont want to pay Bomar anything, and wont if I can help it! But I expect I shall have to. If I do, I'll be slim when I go "ter hum".

Last Saturday, while in Spartanburg, I conversed with several M.D.'s on the subject of studying Medicine. I got some varied advice. One told me to get a Medical Compend. Another told me to study Anatomy. Another, and doubtless the best of the whole lot advised me to go to a Medical College. I can't follow his advice, as there is business which prevents me. That Business is to make money to pay my way. Then, perhaps, I will go. I hope that I shall have good health, and shall try hereafter to pay strict attention to the Laws of health, as established by nature—our mother.

> "How dear to my heart are the scenes of my childhood,
> When fond recollection presents them to view,
> The orchard, the meadow, the deep-tangled wildwood
> And every loved spot which my infancy knew.
>> The wide-spreading pond, and the mill which
>> stood by it,
> The bridge and the rock where the cataract fell,
> The cot of my father, the dairy house nigh it,
> And e'en the rude bucket which hung in the well." [63]

Well! uneducated people, are the most bigoted, superstitious, hardest headed people in the world! Those folks down stairs believe in ghosts, luck, horse shoes, cloud signs and all other kinds of nonsense, and all the argument in the world couldn't get it out of them. It is useless to argue with such persons. All the eloquence of a Demosthenes, the logic of Plato, the demonstrations of the most learned men in this world, couldn't convince them of the falsity, the absurdity, the utter impossibility and unreasonableness of such things. Verily, education is a great thing, and I would I could quote a quire or two of Mayhew's Universal

63. Quoted from the popular early nineteenth-century poem "The Old Oaken Bucket," by Samuel Woodworth (1785–1842).

Education on the subject, "Education lessens and dissipates the effects of ignorance."[64]

The people don't know words enough for a fellow to carry on a conversation with them. He must reduce his phraseology several degrees lower than that of the first reader, and then all the reason and demonstration has no more effect than a drop of water on a field of dry wheat! "Universal Education" is certainly a much-to-be-wished-for, but, at present, but-little-to-be-hoped-for blessing.

Saturday August 20th 1875. This is the doggondest country I ever saw to teach in. They say they'll pay your board, and then don't do it. They accuse you indirectly of lying, almost of stealing, eavesdrop you, retail every word you say. Eavesdrop you when you're talking to yourself, twist up your words into all sorts of ambiguous meanings, refuse to lend you their mules &c. They are the most suspicious people in the world, good-sized liars, hypocrites, inquisitive little ~~nigger~~ wenches &c. I wouldn't teach here another year for fifty dollars a month.

	C. W. Chesnutt & C R H Cr.[65]		
Feb. 6	Bal Due C. R. H.	14.00	
"	Board	13.00	
"	Cash sent home	10.00	
10	Cash	1.00	
12	"	2.00	
15	"	1.00	
20	"	1.00	
Mar. 6	Board	13.00	
	Salary 2 mos.		60.00
		55.00	60.00

64. Chapter 7 of Mayhew's *Means and Ends of Universal Education* contains a section entitled "Education Dissipates the Evils of Ignorance." Mayhew had listed superstition as one of the principal evils dissipated by education and had educed rural southern blacks as a principal example of superstition.

65. These accounts were kept on two blank pages near the back of the first journal volume. When Chesnutt reached these pages with his later journal entries, he skipped over them and continued. In the manuscript journal, the pages fall in the middle of Chesnutt's expostulation against "uneducated people" (81).

	Cash to bal	5.00	
		60.00	60.00
Apr. 6	Board	13.00	
"	Cash	1.00	
" 13	Cash	5.00	
Mar 27	Paper	.75	
Apr 10	Coat & vest		
17	Cash sent home	10.00	
" "	Salary	.25	30.00
		30.00	30.00

Square! ! Hurrah! !

C. W. C. Acct with C. R. H.

Apr 22nd	Cash for Dutch Dict.	1.50	
" 26th	" Christ in Art	3.50	
" 28th	" bottle medicine	1.00	
May 3rd	" express on C. in A.	1.00	
" 6th	Board	13.00	
" 15th	cash ~~salary~~	9.50	
	salary mo.		30.00
		29.50	30.00
	Biddle	50	
	Bal	30.00	30.00

[Chesnutt's first journal concludes with seven pages of Latin schoolbook exercises done on the blank back pages of this journal in 1879.—*Ed.*]

SECOND JOURNAL, 1877-1881

[Fall 1877]

In beginning this journal I have several things in view. I shall keep a record of any noteworthy events that may occur in my knowledge, a record of my performances as recapitulator in the Literary society,[1] facts concerning teaching which are worthy of preservation; criticisms on men and things, on literature and current events. My principal object is to improve myself in the art of composition. As my penmanship is poor for want of constant practice, by means of frequent writing in this my journal I shall doubtless improve in this respect.

In this book I shall confine myself to no particular subject or order of writing. If a bit of poetry strikes my fancy, or may perhaps be of use to me, I shall immediately insert it. If a scientific fact is new, or particularly impressive, it shall be deemed worthy of a place in my note-book.

As this book is intended only for my own perusal, if I write trash no one will be the worse for it. If I write anything that is worth reading, I, perhaps, shall be the better for it.

Nov. 30th. Well! let us review the events of the day. I rose at six, took a walk up town. All the drug stores were closed, and I could find only one dry-goods store open. There was quite a crowd around the market-house, catering for their breakfasts, I presume. The butchers seem to be flourishing.

1. A Literary Society was formed when the State Colored Normal School was established in Fayetteville in 1877. Chesnutt is now the assistant teacher in this new school, serving under Principal Robert Harris.

After making the desired purchases I came home, built up a fire, and began on my algebra. I had had a good night's rest, and my mind being fresh and clear, I made considerable progress. The part of the subject which I am now studying is somewhat difficult. The properties of the Equations are not hard to understand; the difficulty is in remembering them.

I find it much easier to remember difficult things, after once fairly understanding them, than less difficult ones. The greater amount of thinking which is necessary to comprehend them thoroughly impresses the facts and principles more firmly on the mind.

I had a very good day in school. My classes were not unusually stupid, and made commendable progress. Downstairs the children were well-behaved. After school I went up town and purchased a new umbrella while returning, I met Miss J. P. and H. T., and having more umbrellas than I had any need for I lent them the old one.

To-night I have been reading history. The books at my command give but a meagre outline of ancient history. Still from them I have learned much concerning the ancient history of Babylon, Persia, Assyria, Egypt &c. The history of these countries being contemporaneous, and so many changes and coalitions of these countries lying so near each other renders it exceedingly difficult to remember the dates of the various events narrated. Howbeit, if by reading history one gets a general view of the founding of a government[,] the settlement of a country, the building of a city, and remembers the principal events in the history together with some ideas of the manners and customs of the people, his time has been well-spent. And moreover, if I wish to improve myself in writing and composition, I must write at some other time than ten o'clock at night, for then my body is fatigued, my eyes are tired, my mind is anything but vigorous and clear, and my hand, as this writing indicates, by no means steady. In order to write well a clear head and a steady hand are prerequisites.[2]

2. Chesnutt's attempt to revive his journal in the fall of 1877 proved abortive and ends at this point. What follows is a new effort, separated from this one by almost a full year.

August 13th 78.

The first Book of the Iliad

For me to attempt to discuss or even to comment on the Character of Homer would indeed be presumption, when so many great writers have gone over the ground before me. Although every undergraduate has criticised him, though all his real and imaginary beauties have been pointed out, though mountains of paper and rivers of ink have been sacrificed to his memory, yet there may still remain some reflections on his style, or some criticism on his heroes, some bright spot which has not been overflowed by those rivers of ink, or buried under those mountains of paper.

The first line of the first book tells us the subject of the poem—"Achilles' wrath"—which by the will of Jove was the source of more misfortune to the Greeks than all their previous troubles combined; tis true they had besieged Troy for nine years; but no glorious deeds of arms had been performed, no great heroes had fallen, and the whole galaxy of Grecian wisdom and valor is presented to us.

We will follow the course of the narrative, and make such remarks as may be suggested to us in passing. [Here Chesnutt begins a recounting of the first three books of *The Iliad* in Pope's translation that fills forty-six journal pages. This protracted plot summary is omitted here except for the following three entries, which register more general reflections.—*Ed.*]

[From the commentary on book 1:] The Gods are but little or no improvement on their subject mortals. Their characters we have seen. As to their personal habits, they sleep, they drink, they laugh at the awkward Vulcan, they quarrel among themselves, and in the course of the work they lie and cheat just like mortals. The standard of Grecian morality was low, which could permit men to worship such corrupt and partial deitys, but perhaps they worshipped them more from fear than from love. The worship of the Greek was not that of a Christian who loves his God, but that of the slave who cringes obsequiously to a capricious and tyrannical master, who one minute loads them with favors and the next strips them of everything and dismisses them in disgrace.

[From the commentary on book 2:] The Greeks were aristocratic democrats, for if a "clamorous vile plebeian rose," ["]with reproof he checked or blows." He asserts the divine right and supreme power of kings, and wisely speaks of that worst of all tyrants an usurping crowd.

[From the commentary on book 3:] Yesterday while reading the ante-Homeric history of Troy as given in Dwight's Mythology,[3] we were struck by the story of Iphigenia, and its remarkable resemblance to the scriptural account of the offering of Isaac. The resemblance of many of these legends to the stories of Bible History, as that of Deucalion and Pyrrha, Prometheus, Iphigenia and others that could be pointed out, only serve to show us that all men come from a common stock and that those events which occured prior to the dispersion of Babel and shortly afterward, were formerly known to them all, and as Indian and Chinese traditions tell us, were corrupted by the lapse of time and the ignorance of writing[,] and by the addition with which the imagination of different generations adorned them became the improbable legends which are preserved to us in classical literature.

October 7th 1878. I am almost afraid to write what I intend to do, for if I carry out my plan no better than I have three-fourths of the many that I have made, I will not get more than a few pages. But as I have been encouraged and stimulated by my late reading of Dr. Todd's invaluable "Student's Manual",[4] which contains so much sound advice, expressed in elegant language, and illustrated by so many learned quotations and illustrious examples, that it is a pleasure to the scholar to read it, and of incalculable value to the student who will endeavor to profit by it.

The following are some of the quotations which he uses. Of

---

3. Mary Ann Dwight's *Grecian and Roman Mythology,* published around 1850, was available in special school editions in the 1870s.

4. The often-reprinted *Student's Manual: Designed by Specific Directions to Aid in Forming and Strengthening the Intellectual and Moral Character and Habits of the Student,* by Rev. John Todd, was first published in the 1830s and revised in 1854. Chesnutt's quotations from this advice manual come from chapters 2 and 3, "Habits" and "Study."

many the authors are not named and my knowledge of Latin is not sufficient to supply them.

Every man is fitted by nature for some certain pursuit in life, or at least has the power of excelling in some one thing, when he would perhaps never be more than a respectable failure in any other. "Non omnes omnia possumus."[5]

One of the most distinguished scholars of our country has as his motto, the picture of a mountain, with a man at its base, his hat and coat beside him, and a pickaxe in his hand, and as he digs stroke by stroke his patient look corresponds with his words, "Peu et peu." Little by little.

Patience! Be diligent but thorough in your studies. "Ferret taurum qui tulit vitulam." He who would carry the ox must every day shoulder the calf.

Continued efforts. "Gutta cavat lapidem, non vi, sed saepe caedendo."[6] —Luther's reply when asked, how, in the midst of such an active and laborious life, he could complete a perfect translation of the bible—"Nulla dies sine versu".[7]

Lord Macaulay considered Voltaire's history of Charles XII, a model history.[8] I am reading it in the original, and will occasionally transcribe a choice thought in this my note book.

"Il y a bien peu de souverains dont on dût écrire une histoire particulière. —Les princes qui ont le plus de droit à l'immortalité sont ceux qui ont fait quelque bien aux hommes — Telle est la miserable faiblesse des hommes, qu'ils regardent avec admiration ceux qui ont fait du mal d'une manière brillante, et qu'ils parleront souvent plus voluntiers de déstructeur d'une empire que de celui qui l'a fondé."[9] —

---

5. "Everyone is not capable of everything."
6. "The drop hollows out the stone not by force but by repeated striking."
7. "No day without its verse; a verse a day."
8. Voltaire's *Histoire de Charles XII* was published in 1731. A comment inserted later adds: "Lord M. praised Voltaire's C. XII, but Thucydides came nearest to the ideal of a historian."
9. "There are few rulers who deserve a history. The princes who have the greatest right to immortality are those who have done some good for men — Such is the miserable weakness of men that they admire those who have done harm

Oct. 8. I have not only finished my appointed task for today, but have read fifty lines of Virgil in addition. The following passages I write, not that I fully appreciate their beauties, but because I wish to remember them.

The first is a description of the *monstrum* or omen, which warned Aeneas to leave the Island of Crete, to which he had come after leaving Thrace.

> "Nox erat et terris animalia somnus habebat;
> Effigies sacrae divum Phrygiique Penates,
> Quos mecum a Troia mediisque ex ignibus urbis
> Extuleram, visi ante oculos adstare iacentis
> In somnis, multo manifesti lumine, qua se
> Plena per insertas fundebat luna fenestras;" [10]

"Si quelque prince et quelque ministre trouvaient dans cette ouvrage des vérités désagreables qu'ils souviennent qu'étant hommes publics, ils doivent compte au public de leurs actions; et c'est à se prix qu'ils achètent leur grandeur; que l'histoire est un témoin, et non un flatteur; et *que le seul moyen d'obliger les hommes à dire du bien de nous, c'est d'en faire.*" [11]

"Nous aimons la vérité; mais l'ancien proverbe dit, "Toutes vérités ne sont pas bonnes à dire." [12] ——Voltaire

---

in a brilliant fashion, and will often rather speak of the destroyer of an empire than of its founder."

10. "It was night and on earth sleep held the living world. The sacred images of the Gods, the Phrygian Penates, whom I had borne with me from Troy out of the midst of the burning city, seemed as I lay in slumber to stand before my eyes, clear in the flood of light, where the full moon streamed through the inset windows" (*Aeneid* III.147–52, Loeb translation). In journal entries dated October 8–16 Chesnutt goes on to copy several passages from books 3 and 4, the section of *The Aeneid* he is studying at this time, as well as from Cicero's Catiline Oration.

11. "If some prince or minister should find disagreeable truths in this work let them remember that being public men, they are answerable to the public for their actions; that this is the price at which they purchase their greatness; that history is a witness, not a flatterer; *and that the only way to oblige men to speak well of us is to do well.*"

12. "We love the truth, but the ancient proverb says 'Not all truths are good to say.'"

————Voltaire was born in 1694. He received a careful education, and was one of the most copious and versatile of French writers. "He was" says a French author, "one of our greatest poets; the most brilliant, the most elegant, the most fertile, of our prose writers. There is not in the literature of any country, whether in prose or in verse, an author who has written on so many opposite kinds of subjects, and has so consistently displayed a superiority in all of them." He was a Deist, and in the opinion of good men, made himself notorious for his writings against Christianity.

Oct 11th.

> ———— "Horrificus iuxta tonat Aetna ruinis,
> Interdumque atram prorumpit ad aethera nubem,
> Turbine fumantem piceo et candente favilla,
> Attolitque globos flammarum et sidera lambit;
> Interdum scopulos avolsaque viscera montis
> Erigit eructans, liquefactaque saxa sub auras
> Cum gemitu glomerat, fundoque exaestuat imo.
> Fama est, Enceladi semustum flumine corpus
> Urgeri mole hac ingentemque insuper Aetnam
> Impositam, ruptis flammam exspirare caminis,
> Et fessum quotiens mutet latus, intremere omnem
> Murmere Trinacriam et caelum subtextere fumo.["] [13]
>   Aen[eid] III.571

The critics have severely censured that metaphor in the above passage, which represents the mountain as "belching up its bowels with a groan,["] "eructans avolsa viscera cum genitu."

––––––––––––

It is not in keeping with the sublime character of the subject;

13. "But near at hand Aetna thunders with terrifying crashes, and now hurls forth to the sky a black cloud, smoking with pitch-black eddy and glowing ashes, and uplifts balls of flame and licks the stars—now violently vomits forth rocks, the mountain's uptorn entrails, and whirls molten stone skyward with a roar, and boils up from its lowest depths. The story runs that Enceladus' form, scathed by the thunderbolt, is weighed down by that mass, and mighty Aetna, piled above, from its burst furnaces breathes forth flame; and ever as he changes his weary side all Trinacria moans and trembles, veiling the sky in smoke" (Loeb translation).

the introduction of mean ideas in sublime writing has the effect of spoiling the charm.

Oct 12th. "Quand on écrit l'histoire, il faut n'être d'aucun pays, et dépouiller tout esprit de parti."—*Voltaire*[14]

> "As unto the bow the cord is
> So unto the man is woman
> Though she bend him, she obeys him
> Though she draws him, yet she follows
> Useless each without the other!"
> —Longfellow[15]

C. W. Chesnutt.

Oct. 12th 1878

I do not think that I will ever forget my Latin. The labor I spend in trying to understand it thoroughly, and the patience which I am compelled to exercise in clearing up the doubtful or difficult points, furnishes[,] it seems to me, as severe a course of mental discipline as a college course would afford. I would above all things like to enjoy the ~~privilege~~ advantages of a good school, but must wait for a future opportunity.

—In some things I seem to be working in the dark. I have to feel my way along, but by perseverance I manage to make better headway than many who have the light; and besides, like the Edmund Dantes in Dumas' "Monte Cristo,"[16] I have become accustomed to the darkness. As I have been thrown constantly on my own resources in my solitary studies, I have acquired some degree of *self-reliance*. As I have had no learned professor or obliging classmate to construe the hard passages, and work the difficult problems, I have "*persevered*" till I solved them myself.

—I love music. I live in a town where there is *some* musical cul-

14. "When one writes history one must be of no country and cast off all partisan spirit."

15. This once-famous passage comes from part 10 of Henry Wadsworth Longfellow's "Hiawatha."

16. Alexandre Dumas père's *Count of Monte Cristo* was published in both Paris and New York in 1846.

ture; I have studied and practiced till I can understand and appreciate good music, but I never hear what little there is to be heard. I have studied German and have no one to converse with but a few Jewish merchants[17] who can talk nothing but business. As to procuring instruction in Latin, French, German, or Music, that is entirely out of the question. First class teachers would not teach a "nigger" and I would have no other sort.

I will go to the North, where, although the prejudice sticks, like a foul blot on the fair scutcheon of American liberty, yet a man may enjoy these privileges if he has the money to pay for them. I will live down the prejudice, I will crush it out. I will show to the world that a man may spring from a race of slaves, and yet far excel many of the boasted ruling race. If I can exalt my race, if I can gain the applause of the good, and the approbation of God, the thoughts of the ignorant and prejudiced will not concern me. If a man be too proud, too selfconceited, or so blinded by prejudice as not to recognize and honor true merit wherever discovered, I want not his good opinion. Let him reserve it for those whom it will please or displease!

Style. —Dr Blair   Lecture X[18]
All the qualities of good style may be ranged under two heads, perspicuity and ornament. —Perspicuity is the fundamental quality of style. Says Quintillian: "Oratio debet negligenter quoque audientibus esse aperta; ut in animum audientis sicut sol in oculos, etiam in eum non intendatur, occurat. Quare non solum ut intelligere possit, sed ne omnino possit non intelligere currandum."[19] —Difficulty of subject is no excuse for want of

17. The 1880 census registers several foreign-born and apparently Jewish merchants in Fayetteville: Simon Brandt, George Rosenthal, [illegible first name] Strouse, Mat. Scholssburg, and Nathan Cohen—the first four German-born, the last born in England. Judging by the census records, this group formed one of the few sectors of the town's population, white or black, not born in North Carolina of Carolina-born parents.

18. This and the subsequent entries form a precis of Hugh Blair's *Lectures on Rhetoric and Belles Lettres* (1783), a standard text in American schools in the eighteenth and nineteenth centuries. This discussion is from "Lecture X: On Style—Perspicuity and Precision."

19. "Discourse ought always to be obvious, even to the most careless and most negligent hearer; so that the sense shall strike his mind, as the light of the sun

perspicuity. Whatever a man conceives clearly, he can express distinctly; and on no subject ought a man to write, upon which his ideas are not clear. —Perspicuity is not to be considered as a mere negative virtue or freedom from defect; it is a degree of positive beauty.

—Perspicacity, considered with respect to words and phrases, requires three qualities in them, *purity, propriety,* and *precision.*

——— Purity is the use of such words, and such constructions, as belong to the idiom of the language which we speak. It requires that we should avoid words or phrases from foreign languages, when we have a sufficient store of words in our own language to express our ideas correctly; that we should avoid obsolete, or new-coined words, and all words used without good authority.

— Propriety is the selection of such words and phrases in the language, as the best and most established usage has appropriated to those ideas which we intend to express by them. It requires also the avoidance of vulgarisms or low expressions. —Dean Swift,[20] a most correct writer[,] valued himself much on using no words but such as were of native birth— Our author gives no exact definition of precision, but goes on to illustrate it at some length. In substance he says, that "Precision requires a writer to express his meaning fully and distinctly, and to introduce no superfluous thought, no trifling or misplaced side circumstance which would distract the attention of the reader from the main idea. — The great source of a loose style, in opposition to precision, is the injudicious use of words termed synonymous. Upon the proper use of these words depend both propriety and precision, and perspicuity is greatly injured by their misapplication, which is very frequent among some writers. — "To unite copiousness and precision, to be flowing and graceful, and at the same time correct and exact in the choice of every word, is, no doubt, one of the highest and most difficult attainments in writing."

---

does our eyes, though they are not directed upwards to it. We must study, not only that every hearer may understand us, but that it shall be impossible for him not to understand us" (Blair's translation).

20. Jonathan Swift (1667–1745), dean of St. Patrick's Cathedral in Dublin, author of *Gulliver's Travels* and *A Modest Proposal* among other works.

Blair's Rhetoric—Structure of Sentences—Lect XI

Aristotle[']s definition of a sentence: "A form of speech which has a beginning and an end within itself and is of such length as to be easily comprehended at once."

— First variety that occurs in the consideration of sentences is the distinction of long and short ones. With regard to this quality the French make a very just distinction of style, into *style periodique,* where the sentences are composed of several members linked together, and not bringing out the full sense till the close, and *style coupè*[,] which forms the sense into short independent propositions, each complete within itself.

The first gives an air of gravity and dignity to composition, the latter is more lively and striking.

— But in every species of composition the great rule is to intermix them — We cannot be too strict in our attention to the construction of sentences — By observing the following rules we acquire the habit of expressing ourselves with perspicuity and elegance: and if a disorder occurs in some one of our sentences, we immediately see where it lies, and are able to rectify it.

The properties essential to a perfect sentence are 1. Clearness and precision. (2) Unity. 3. Strength. 4. Harmony.

— Ambiguity arises either from a wrong choice of words, or a wrong collocation of them. — In arranging the words in a sentence pay strict attention to the rules of grammar. Place the members which are most nearly related, in such a position that their mutual relation will be clearly indicated.

— Most errors in this respect arise from the wrong collocation of such adverbs as *only, wholly*[,] *at least,* &c. —; From the improper disposition of the relative pronouns, which[,] what, whose, and of all those particles which express the construction of the parts of speech. We cannot be too accurate here. — Avoid the too frequent repetition of pronouns when they refer to different persons. — Unity is that quality of a well-arranged sentence which binds all the members together and makes it a single proposition.

Unity requires: 1., that the scene should be changed as little as possible during the course of the sentence. — (2) Never crowd into one sentence things which have so little connection that they could be divided into several — 3. Keep clear of all parentheses in the middle of the sentence (4) Bring it to a full and perfect close ——

The importance of ~~an~~ ideas ~~is~~ measured by men ~~in proportion to~~ the capacity of their own minds.[21] An insignificant thought fills the mind of an ignorant or narrow minded person, and of course appears immeasurably vast to him, when it would scarcely occupy an appreciable space in the mind of a man of broad and comprehensive views. — Following this we might suppose that great ideas would be dwarfed by their reception into small minds, but it is not so, for the small minds never entertain them. Great thoughts are like the wooden horse of the Greeks which could not be got in at the gates of Troy; but unlike the walls of that city, the barriers of ignorance cannot be broken down to admit them.

————————

————Nothing will sooner show us the folly and injustice of prejudice than being ourselves subjected to it.

——of any kind—

————There are two theories concerning the second coming of our Lord. The express and oft reiterated declarations of Scripture leave no room for doubt as to the fact of this Second Advent. "This same Jesus which is taken up from you into heaven shall so come in like manner as ye have seen him go into heaven."[22] The question between the two schools of thought in the church is, not "Will he come again?" but, "How and when will he come?" The two theories of his coming involve two conceptions of Christianity. The one is the development hypothesis as applied to future events; the other involves belief in an hypothesis of spiritual cataclysm. — The development theory is that of conservative orthodoxy. By the gospel and the other instruments of improvement, by the same means that have been, and are now in operation, the world will gradually grow better and better; and will become a Christian world as England and America are now Christian nations. And when the world is thus

21. Chesnutt has renumbered the words in this sentence to indicate the preferred revision: "Men measure the importance of ideas by the capacity of their own minds."
22. The quotation is from Acts 1:11.

perfected, He will come, and present it as a shining jewel for His father's crown. His coming will be gradual. The virgins may trim their lamps but there is no need to watch, until the cry goes forth, Behold the Bridegroom cometh, for we know that he cannot come, except in his spiritual nature, for many centuries yet.

The other theory is that called by its friends Second Coming, and by its enemies Second Adventism. It does not consider Christianity as the hope of a universal salvation, but as a witness to the nation. Christ is not garnering his grain but winnowing it, He is not perfecting his race, but selecting from it the materials out of which a future race is to be formed. He may come at any moment; the Scriptures do not warrant our deferring his coming to a period in the far future, no more than it does our expecting him tomorrow. We should be ready for him at any time. He will come in all his majesty and sweep the wicked from the earth, and then shall establish that blessed Millenium, the thousand years of peace.

(Abstract of an Editorial in "Christian Union" Nov. 1878. Presume the author is Rev. Lyman Abbot.)[23]

Dr. Blair—Lecture XIV—Figurative Language.

In his former lectures our author has considered one of the great branches of the qualities of style, perspicuity, both in single words and the structure of sentences. With respect to the other branch, ornament, he introduces the subject by the lecture on the "Origin and Nature of Figurative Language", of which a few of the leading thoughts are contained in the following abstract.

Figures of speech may be simply defined as those forms of expression, in which one thought is clothed in the language of another, by which means the writer points out some analogy between the two.

23. The *Christian Union* was a widely influential journal of liberal Congregationalist thought in post–Civil War America. Lyman Abbott (1835–1922), who succeeded Henry Ward Beecher as minister of the Plymouth Congregational Church in Brooklyn and as editor of the *Christian Union,* helped broadcast a version of liberal Protestantism compatible with the theory of evolution in *The Theology of an Evolutionist* and other works.

Figures of speech are not artificial or unnatural, as the many treatises on the subject, and the attention which rhetoricians have always bestowed upon them, might lead us to suppose. This is so far from being the case, that on many occasions they are both the most natural and the most common method of uttering our sentiments. Savage nations use them plentifully, and in the ordinary conversation, even of the most ignorant, they are very frequently employed.[24]

Our author dispenses with the many subdivisions into which rhetoricians have divided figures of speech, and of their cumbrous nomenclature[.] He makes but few divisions, for he considers that the use of figures is more natural than artificial and that their choice and application should be left to the impulses of a cultivated imagination, rather than dictated by any arbitrary rules. — It does not follow from this that rules are of no service. All science arises from observations on practice. Practice has always gone before method and rule; but method and rule have afterwards improved and perfected practice in every art. And to know the Principles which underly propriety in speech, cannot fail to assist and direct a proper choice. — Tropes mean words used as figures; figures of thought are those in which the figure consists in the thought which may be preserved even if the language should be changed. The distinction, however, is vague and general, and is of no practical use, so that we remember that figurative language always imports some coloring which arises from the imagination or from passion, and is expressed in our style. — A great deal of unnecessary attention has been bestowed upon this subject, which has drawn

24. At this point, at the bottom of a page, Chesnutt writes in the following poem before continuing his abstract of Blair's *Rhetoric:*

> The solitary student, by the midnight oil,
> ~~His books around him, still pursues his mental toil,~~
> Bends over his books in unremitting toil
> Dives in the sea of knowledge, and brings forth
> Shells of rare beauty, gems of priceless worth.
> And finds in their possession a reward
> ~~Of~~ far ~~more value~~ greater than the richest miser's hoard.
>   C. C.

Chesnutt later wrote a second verse for this poem. See p. 103.

to its study much labor which should have been given to other parts of composition. For however numerous and definite the rules may be, however great may be your knowledge of them, remember that the figure is only the dress; the sentiment is the body, and substance.

And moreover, a writer's chief dependence must be on himself, for no author wishes to be a servile imitator, and good sense, and certainly a cultivated taste will be sufficient to detect the improper use of figures, while a lively imagination is necessary to supply them.

> It was in the joyful spring-time
> That first I saw the light
> And raised from earth my tiny head
> To greet the sunbeam bright.
>
> The husbandman had plowed his land
> And sowed the yellow grain
> And left it to the genial sun,
> And the softening spring-time rain.
>
> Deep in the dark damp womb of earth
> For many a weary day
> Without a ray of light or hope
> In deep despair I lay
>
> Till nature pitied my sad fate
> And sent the melting rain
> Which broke the shell that held me
> Prisoned in the stubborn grain.
>
> She sent a sunbeam from on high
> A sunbeam warm and bright
> Which pierced the superincumbent earth
> And taught me of the light
>
> It roused my dormant energies
> To seek the wished-for day,
> And force my passage upward
> Through the opposing wall of clay
>
> Joyful I raised my drooping head
> And strove with all my might

The sunbeam cheered me on my way,
And soon I reached the light

I saw the sun! the radiant sun!
That sun I long had sought
And basked with rapture in the warmth
That many sunbeams brought

I saw the plants and trees around;
Above, the bright blue sky
My quickened heart within me leapt,
In praise to Him on high

I grew and flourished, day by day
Still rising, higher, higher,
My soul is not content with earth
To heaven I aspire!

6   My green leaves spread themselves abroad
And drink the summer air,
I stand upright in all my pride.
What work of art so fair?

7   A powdered tassel crowns my head,
The shooting ears appear,
And soon adorn their pointed tops
With crests of golden hair

8   No noxious weeds absorb my strength
The farmer keeps them clear
He plucks away the noisome worm,
And guards the swelling ear.

9   But ah! this state of happiness
Will not forever last
The brightest sky with gloomy clouds
At length is overcast.

10   My sturdy stalk will soon grow dry
My golden hair grow brown
My bright green leaves will droop and die
And strew the earth around

11   But though my stalk shall suffer death
My seed ~~can perish never~~ will still remain

The germ is still within the grain
And may grow ~~on forever~~ on a thousand years

O man learn from the stalk of maize
A lesson thou shouldst heed
Will He who keeps the plant, permit
His "little ones" to need?[25]

———————

Some chords there are in the human heart,
That "harp of a thousand strings,"
~~That nought~~ Which only the hand of love
    alone can strike
And make their music ring.
While others may thoughtlessly rudely jar
And with dissonance harsh the melody mar,
Love is the master whose matchless skill
Can make even discord with harmony thrill.

                    —Dec 1878

The human heart is like a mighty harp
Whose thousand strings give forth a thousand tones
Which always, as they are combined produce
Or jarring discords or the sweetest sounds.
Some tones are deep bass notes and seldom touched
               day
But ~~when~~ in the times of danger or distress—
When truth opposed demands the martyr's blood
When tyrants have aroused the people's wrath
When cruel war's red hand is lifted high—
The deepest notes are sounded, and inspire
The soul with courage to heroic deeds.

                    —Jan. 1879

25. The stanza numbers indicate Chesnutt's intended reordering of the verses in question, a reordering this transcription has put into practice. In the manuscript journal the stanza now numbered 11 is followed by the stanza numbered 10. Stanza 9 is written across the page and referred to by a marginal note above stanza 11: "see next page." Chesnutt apparently neglected five stanzas on the preceding manuscript page when counting his verses. A later hand has lightly numbered the first five stanzas of this poem, neglected to number the next five, then numbered the next three stanzas 6, 7, and 8.

The bells are ringing merrily,
　The fires are blazing cheerily,
　　And throughout the land,
　　　In chorus grand
　　Ten thousand voices are lifted high
　In praise of him who came to die
　　　For sinful man.
　　　　　Christmas 1878.

My Books

Have you ever been in my library? Have you read any of my books? They are many, and in a large apartment. If you should travel day and night, by the swiftest means of conveyance, for three whole months you could only make the circuit of its walls.

As for the books, you would not have time to look at them. You might see some of their handsome covers and gilt edges as you hurried past, but you could have no idea of your contents.[26]

Out in the crowded streets at night
When the gas is lit, and the way is bright
And the busy stores look gay,
Men are hurrying to and fro,
On business and pleasure the[y] come and go
And press along the way.

Merchants and Bankers with lips compressed
And brows contracted that know no rest
From the throbbing brains within,
Who are ceaselessly dreaming "of bulls" and "bears"
Of profit and loss and business cares
And the wealth that they shall win.

Bustling matrons with buxom forms
And huge market baskets upon their arms
In search of groceries bound;
With juvenile escorts attached to their skirts
To protect them, you know, from the insults and hurts
That are incident to the town.

26. Penciled marginal note: "Manuscript misplaced."

Here is a lover with sparkling eyes;
He has distanced his rivals and won the prize
He had fixed his heart upon—
So with step elastic and heart elate,
He hurries along at a rapid rate
To visit his darling one.

Here is a church—the Temple of God—
The organ is pealing in anthem loud
(1) And the lights are bright within
But many pass by without giving a look
To the minister who from the holy book
(2) Is offering pardon for sin
(1) (but the congregation is small) (2) (pardon to all).

Here is a grog-shop—the Temple of Sin
"And many there be who enter therein"
      Of the crowd who the church have past
Nine of the ten who hurried by
With quickened step and averted eye
      Enter the grog-shop at last.

Student   2nd Verse[27]

The shells are pleasant thoughts and fancies sweet
Which now and then [the] student's eye may meet
The pearls those truths of nature and of art
Which nerve the intellect and warm the heart.
Toil, only toil, these prizes can obtain,
The faithful student labors not in vain.

"Our desires are the presentiments of the faculties which lie within us—the precursors of those things which we are capable of performing. That which we would be and that which we desire, present themselves to our imagination, about us, and in the future: we prove our aspiration after an object which we already secretly possess. It is thus that an intense anticipation transforms a real possibility into an imaginary reality. When

27. A continuation of the poem begun on p. 98.

such a tendency is decided in us, at each stage of our development a portion of our primitive desire accomplishes itself, under favorable circumstances by direct means: and in unfavorable circumstances by some more circuitous route, from which, however, we never fail to reach the straight road again[.]"

Goethe[28]

"I think—though John rarely betrayed it—he had had strongly this presentiment of future power, which may be often noticed in men who have carved out their own fortunes[.]"
"They have in them the instinct to rise; and a surely as water finds its own level, so do they, from however low a source, ascend to theirs."

Mrs Mulock (Craik) in "Jno. Halifax"[29]

April 23—1879. Some think it is a wise thing to keep a diary; others think it very foolish, but, in my opinion, very few ever try it for a sufficient time to ascertain which of the two views is really correct. It seems to me that a record of the most important events in one's own life, and the results to which they have led, together with the reflections which were suggested by them at the time of their occurrence, would be useful and entertaining in after life. If writing a lesson helps to learn it why may not writing a good resolution help to keep it? Besides, we frequently think of things we would like to remember, but cannot recall to mind distinctly, and in such cases a written record is invaluable. For example, I wish just now, to remember the date of my interview with Professor Ladd (J. J.)[30] at the Fayetteville

28. From Johann Wolfgang von Goethe's *Dichtung und Wahrheit,* translated as *The Autobiography of Goethe, Truth and Poetry: From my Life,* volume 1, part II, book 9.

29. The highly moral novel *John Halifax, Gentleman,* by the English author Mrs. Dinah Maria Mulock Craik (1826–1887), remained an esteemed item on the list of respectable books in America throughout the Victorian period.

30. When the State Colored Normal School was founded at Fayetteville, the state government simultaneously created a normal school for the training of white teachers within the University of North Carolina. The Vermont-born John J. Ladd, a graduate of Brown University and formerly the superintendent of schools at Staunton, Virginia, became the chief instructor in this program— and an arbiter, therefore, of Chesnutt's achievements as they would have been measured had his race not excluded him from that school.

hotel last fall, but cannot. The conversation I remember well. It was like discharging the matter from an old sore. I had a sympathetic ear; a man of Northern birth and education. I told him of my acquirements and my aims, and he was astonished. I read a selection from Virgil, in order that he might criticise my Latin pronunciation. To my surprise and delight it was perfect, and my labor had not been in vain. He declared that he had never met a youth who, at my age and with my limited opportunities for instruction, had made such marked and rapid progress in learning. He encouraged me to continue my studies, and tendered me a job of reporting when I should have mastered Phonography. I read some of my poetical productions, and he admired them very much, declaring that I had poetical taste and talent. From that time I have worked with increased ardor, and with a greater confidence in my own powers.

But I do not place too high a value upon the Professor's opinions. I hope to pass examination at a bar of a higher tribunal, that of the public; but before that can take place there must come long years of hard work, and patient plodding. But I am not at all discouraged. A few weeks ago I sent a letter and some bits of verse to the Christian Union.[31] I have never heard from them, and as I requested the Editor to consign them to the waste-basket (which he would have done anyway) if they were not worth publishing, I presume he did so; but as they were puerile productions, and sent to a paper of high literary character they were not fit for it. The editor of our Gazette offered to publish them, but my object was not to see them in print, but to find out whether they were worth printing or not.

—I had the pleasure of a long conversation with Dr. Haigh, when he was waiting for the advent of my little Ethel into this "sinful world."[32] He thinks I can succeed in the North, for there are more opportunities, and less prejudice. What they want there is ability[,] and this qualification, with energy and perse-

31. On the *Christian Union,* see p. 97 and 106–8.
32. Chesnutt's first child was born in late April 1879. He had married Susan Perry, a fellow teacher at the Howard School, on June 6, 1878. Dr. T. D. Haigh (1829–1908), a white physician and member of a prominent Fayetteville family, attended Chesnutt's wife during the delivery of Ethel. He served as chairman of the Board of Managers of the State Colored Normal School when Chesnutt was the school's principal.

verance will carry a man through. I told him that my object was to obtain my proper standing in society, (and that to be judged according to my merit) and he only expressed the same belief that I have had for some time,—that when a young man starts out in life with a purpose, and works *for* that purpose he is more than apt to accomplish it.

I will go to the Metropolis, or some other large city, and like Franklin[,] Greely and many others,[33] there will I stick. I will live somehow, but live I will, and work. I can get employment in some literary avocation, or something leading in that direction. I depend principally upon my knowledge of stenography, which I hope will enable me to secure a position on the staff of some good newspaper, and then,—work, work, work! I will trust in God and work. I will test the social problem. I will see if it's possible for talent, wealth, genius to acquire social standing and distinction.

This work I shall undertake not for myself alone, but for my children, for the people with whom I am connected—for humanity!

He who would master others should first learn to master himself. *So will Ich strebe zu thun, mitt Gottes Hilfe.*[34]

Copy of a letter sent to the Christian Union
April 79. Editors[,] Christian Union

I have just finished reading the paragraph in last week's Union, in regard to the Jubilee singers,[35] and their concert at Nashville, and I cannot longer refrain from thanking you for the interest which is displayed by you through your invaluable

33. Benjamin Franklin (1706–1790) and the journalist and political leader Horace Greeley (1811–1872) were major figures in the mythology of the self-made man. The story of Greeley's setting out from obscure origins to make a name for himself in the city had been extensively publicized during his unsuccessful presidential campaign in 1872.

34. "So shall I strive to do, with God's help."

35. Begun as a device to raise funds for the newly founded Fisk University, the Fisk Jubilee Singers toured the United States and Europe beginning in 1871, singing spirituals and slave songs in concertized versions. Enormously admired in the North, they formed a principal means of white access to African-American culture in the postbellum years.

paper, in the advancement of the colored people, in common with your enlightened and Christian views upon all the great subjects that come before the public.

Some weeks ago one of your correspondents took offence at your remarks on the election frauds, and the intimidation of voters in some of the Southern States. In the course of the letter he says, if I mistake not, "Let the colored people protect themselves", and speaks of the "intense white light of criticism" which would protect them in the exercise of their lawful rights.

Now whether it is the effect of this "intense white light of criticism["] or not, in North Carolina, the state where I reside, the colored people have, for several years, had little or no trouble in the exercise of their political rights. In most parts of the state ~~they~~ we have a fair proportion of jurors. The white people seem to be very well disposed toward us, the school fund is distributed in proportion to the number of scholars of each race, and the state has established a Normal school at Fayetteville. The institution is in the hands of colored teachers, ~~among whom is your correspondent.~~ I take pleasure in saying that many of the Southern States could well take example from N.C. in her attitude toward the Colored people.

I am glad to accept the incident at Nashville as a hopeful sign, and one that "marks an era in the progress of the colored people toward recognition", and cherish a fond hope that, in this age of improvements, this country of rapid changes, the time of that recognition is not very far off.

It has long been a subject for discussion among the colored people in this country "whether the existing prejudice against them was due to their color or their condition in life", and the general opinion has been that it was mostly the latter. But now that slavery has been abolished, and the South is beginning to see what the North has long known, that to oppress the colored people is neither to the interest nor honor of our Republic; now that these people are in a fair way for improving their worldly condition, may it not be hoped that this unreasonable prejudice against them will finally disappear.

The security of property encourages the acquisition of real estate, and as the colored people constitute the majority of the laboring class in the South, not only in the more menial employments, but in the mechanical trades, it is from them that the influential "middle class" will be largely recruited in the future. The colored people are eager for improvement, and in this and other states of the South, their educational facilities are as good as those which are provided at public expense for the whites. It is true that there's a scarcity of *good* teachers, but there are now schools, which are supported either at public expense, or by various missionary or benevolent societies within comparatively easy access to those who wish to fit themselves for teachers, and to the credit of the Colored People be it said, they are generally well attended.

The more intelligent portion of the colored people of the South are mostly engaged in teaching, or the ministry, and while we are inclined to think it a hardship that these are the only professions we can enter with much prospect of success, it is doubtless best so, for it is there that the labor is most needed, and will accomplish most good.

The Colored People will advance. They have obstacles to encounter, but they will overcome them; they have a work to accomplish, and they will achieve it!

I believe that the American People will recognize worth[,] ability or talent, wherever it shows itself, and that as the colored people, as a class, show themselves worthy of respect and recognition, the old prejudice will vanish, or wear away, and the Colored Man in America will be considered, not as a separate race, not as a stranger and a pariah, but as a friend and brother; that he may become a strong pillar in the Temple of American Liberty, and be "bone of one bone, flesh of one flesh" with the New American Nation! [36]

An account of a visit to the City of Washington, Capital of the United States of America, situated on the Potomac River, in the Dist. of Columbia. By Charles Waddell Chesnutt, Professor of Reading, Writing, Spelling &c in the State Colored Normal School of N C.[37]

MDCCCLXXIX

---

36. Some time later Chesnutt entered the following note after this entry: ("This letter was not published. I am glad of it, it was not worth publishing.")

37. Chesnutt made his visit to Washington, D.C., in the early summer of 1879. Here as elsewhere in his journals an eruption of anxious aspiration coincides with the arrival of a school vacation.

It is a difficult task for a man—perhaps the most difficult he could undertake—to form a correct estimate of his own character. It is always easy to criticise others, even when we know little or nothing about them; but to judge ourselves, when every act, every trait of character, every motive is known to us, is a far more arduous undertaking.

Nature has provided every man with an abundance of self-esteem, and this quality is most essential to human happiness. The poet who says

> "O wad some power the giftie gie us
> To see oursel's as ithers see us"[38]

—had his request been granted—would have conferred upon mankind a source of misery which is happily withheld.

Every man looks most attentively upon the favorable side of his own character. When a merchant fails in business, he ascribes it to financial depression, to dishonest debtors—to anything, in fact, except his own carelessness, incapacity, or want of foresight. If a fair reputation is blighted, the fallen one dwells upon the *strength* of the temptation, and not upon his own *weakness*. The ugly man rejoices in the possession of intellectual power, while the beautiful fool is consoled for her dearth of ideas.

It is this natural and universal tendency which renders it so difficult for one to form a correct estimate of his own character; but it is a most desirable quality for one to be able to look back upon any single act or any line of conduct, to analyze the motives which led to it, and the results which have accrued from it, and as nature has not given us this power in a large degree, it is the duty of the wise man to cultivate it, and to acquire such a knowledge of himself that he may be able to at least understand himself thoroughly.

My temperament, as I comprehend it, is a *potpourri* of harmonies and discords, over which I have not yet acquired sufficient power, to make agreeable music. Phrenologically, it is a compound of the sanguine and nervous temperaments. A large degree of energy, perseverance, and fidelity, a quick conscience, and an instinctive aversion to anything mean or dishonest; a

38. From Robert Burns's "To a Louse," one of Chesnutt's favorite poems in his early years.

strong sense of justice, and a great one to wrong or prejudice in any shape. A retired modest disposition, and a decided deficiency in the quality of "brass" or "cheek", as it is variously denominated.

On the other hand, I have a fatal propensity for building air castles—"Aerial Architecture" you might call it—a fault very common to youth. The different professions I have embraced, the plans I have formed for the future could be counted by thousands, and all, in my brilliant imagination, were but so many different paths to the Temple of Fame. I have been Lawyer, Physician, Architect, Farmer, Minister, Teacher, Poet, Musician, Reporter, Editor, Author, Politician, etc, *ad infinitum,* and in each I have risen to the top of my profession.

I have encouraged this dangerous habit too much for my happiness[.] It makes me feel that nothing I possess is good enough, and the spirit of discontent revels in my poor brain. I consider my present employment, unworthy of me, and am therefore tempted to neglect it, even though I live by it. This discontented spirit has had a tendency to make me irritable and I frequently find sharp words on my tongue when I have no intention of using them. I have a carping fault-finding habit, which is very disagreeable to others, ~~and a natural love of luxury~~[.] I am deficient, also, in self-control, which, in impulsive and sanguine temperaments, is, I presume one among the last qualities to be fully developed—if indeed, it is ever *fully* developed.

A close student, the ideas derived from books have been tempered and assimilated to real life, by a considerable experience of men and things—more in fact than is usually possessed by young men of my age.

The result of so many contradictory qualities is to make up a character which is generally respected. When in company or away from home the instinct of self-preservation makes me always try to appear in the best light; at home, where I am not under so much restraint, I find it more difficult to conceal the more objectionable side of my character.

This I believe to be a fair estimate of my own character. In view of this knowledge of it which I possess I am earnestly striving to improve it. A short description of my visit to Washington will illustrate several features of my character.

About a year since I began the study of Phonography. I had

pursued the study some years ago, and took it up again last summer. I made rapid progress, and soon formed the intention of acquiring sufficient skill in the art to become a phonographic Reporter. So I worked hard as could be for eight months and acquired the requisite skills to report sermons nearly, if not quite *verbatim*. Before I was half through learning it, I had determined to seek employment when I had finished my studies in Phonography. I had before engaged myself to report a series of lectures for Professor Ladd this summer, if he secured the appointment as teacher of the white normal school, but I soon began to think that a small matter. I would seek a larger field; I would go North immediately and secure a position as official reporter for Congress or on the staff of some large newspaper. As I acquired greater skill I gave full rein to my exuberant fancy, and indulged my propensity for castle-building to a fearful extent. From the gains I made with my art, I sent Lewis and Andrew[39] to College; gave up my position in the normal school; built a fine house, edited a great Journal, and acquired a world wide reputation. I grew discontented with my situation and considered it merely as a means of acquiring a little filthy lucre. Nevertheless I had just sufficient sense left to keep up appearances, and to engage myself for the next session, though intending to resign it during the summer if I could do better.

I worked hard, worried Susie[40] into a positive dislike for me, reading so much, and at the close of school I packed my valises, and the following week took the train for Washington[,] N.Y. etc. buoyed up with high hopes of success and bright visions of the privileges and rights enjoyed by colored men in the blessed land to which my steps were turned.

I had sufficient prudence however to believe that the prospect was not altogether bright. I knew a good many things about leaving home and several acquaintances of mine had tried the very experiment I was engaged in, and failed miserably. But I had the quite natural vanity to think that as my ability and acquirements were superior to theirs, that my chance for success would be proportionately greater.

The journey to Washington was about as disagreeable as

39. Chesnutt's younger brothers.
40. Chesnutt's wife, Susan Perry Chesnutt.

travelling generally is. The dust and dirt of the R.R. cars, the smoke (of which I had the full benefit, as I traveled second class), the tiresome stoppages, the provoking slowness of some of the trains, the rapacity of porters and luggage boys, all combined to make the journey an infliction which is endured simply because it can't be helped.

Our route lay by Raleigh, Weldon, and Norfolk, and thence by steamer to Washington. Fortunately I made close connection all through; from Ral. to Wel. on an accomodation freight train. The word accomodation, by the way, is a decided misnomer in this connection. The coach which is used is made for this special purpose, and the one originally put on at the opening of the road, has to duty until it wears out. It is generally a small badly furnished box, with dirty floors, dirty windows, and almost invariably a empty water-can, with a battered tin cup to tantalize the thirsty traveller. The wretched victim reads, smokes, counts the rails in fences as the train creeps slowly by[,] stops at every station for a drink, and occasionally gets out and takes a walk of a few miles, and then waits for the train to come up. Before the distance is half travelled he registers a solemn vow that he will ever after travel in the mail-train.

I had bought second-class tickets all along, but thanks to the small number of travellers, or the kindness of the Conductor, or Captain as he is called in the South (such is the mania for titles!) that I was allowed to ride first-class as far as Franklin where we changed cars for Norfolk. But here the passengers were more numerous, and the Conductor more strict, and I was obliged to ride in the 2nd class car. A gentleman from Weldon was in the same predicament, so that I had some company in my exile. It was pleasant enough till we took on about fifty darkies who were going to Norfolk to work on a truck farm. They filled the seats and standing room, and sat in each other's laps for want of seats. As the day was warm and the people rather dirty, the odor may better be imagined than described[.] Although it was nothing to me, I could empathise with my fellow traveller, who stuck his head out of the window, and swore he would never be caught in such a scrape again.

It was a merry crowd however, especially one young fellow who would gravely line out a hymn and then sing it himself, with all the intonations of a camp meeting. His sister, he said, sat in his lap, though the affectionate way in which he embraced her seemed, to our unsophisticated eyes, to render the relationship doubtful, at the least.

As we neared Norfolk the country began to assume a more cultivated and productive appearance. The fields of cabbages, strawberries, garden peas, and potatoes, with the long rows of forcing beds or frames, bespoke the proximity of a good market, and the existence of a few enterprising men. The force law is in operation in Norfolk County, as the open fields showed.[41]

At Norfolk I bought a ticket on the Geo. Leary, a handsome steamer which was carrying a party of "Rechobites"[42] on an excursion to Washington. The boat was roomy and comfortable, the water was smooth, the crowd large, and some of the women were handsome. There was a piano in the ladies cabin, and a string band which discoursed quadrilles for the dancers on the lower deck.

We reached Norfolk at 6 in the morning. I took the 7th St. cars, and soon found my friend W—— in a dirty room in the 6th story of a large house right in the business part of the city. I took him a little by surprise, but was cordially welcomed.

W——'s room was large and comfortable. It was supplied with gas, and water could be had from the hydrant in the fourth story. But this hydrant was so near the water closet, which it supplied, that though the water was good I could never drink it with much relish. The most disagreeable thing about W's situation, was the din, worse than that of a dozen grist mills, which arose from the street below. The pavement was of cobblestones, and the rattle of the cars, and wagons, the tramp of pedestrians, the discordant yells of the newsboys and fruit vendors made up a hideous noise which was very disagreeable to my country-bred ears.

It would require too much space for me to attempt to describe all the sights I saw in Washington. I can only give a mere outline, and the inquisitive reader can refer to the Guide-book for particulars (details.)

I paid several visits to the Capitol, which is as it should be,

41. A marginal note, presumably of a later date, adds here: "no."
42. I have been unable to identify this group or sect, evidently named after a biblical family that practiced asceticism; see Jeremiah 35.

a magnificent structure. It is worthy to be Capitol of a great nation. The tall dome pierces the sky at an altitude of 395 ft, and from its lofty summit the Goddess of Liberty looks down upon the broad land which acknowledges her sway. The architecture of the building is Corinthian, and the vast marble pile is truly imposing. The North and South entrances are flanked by colossal statues; and many others executed by good masters in the highest style of the art, find their places in various niches throughout the building. Historical paintings are placed on the stairways, and around the rotunda. They are mostly battle pieces, representing scenes in the Rev.[,] the War of 1812, and the Mex. war. (According to act of Congress, passed after the late war, no picture of battles or other scenes in the Civil War can be admitted to the Capitol. The reason is obvious.) The Canopy or concave covering of the dome, of cast iron, contains an allegorical painting by Brumidi,[43] which cost $39,000. From below the figures appear of life-size, and the coloring is very chaste, but on ascending the dome to within a few feet of the picture, the figures are large and ugly, and the coloring coarse. But in this the art consists, as they were painted to be viewed from below, a distance of over 300 ft. The gray haired artist is still engaged in decorating the rotunda, and, perched upon a slender scaffold half way up the dome, still plies his brush industriously.

The floors of the halls are of stone mosaic, while the walls are covered with frescoes in elegant designs. The committee rooms, the President's Room, and all the private apartments are sumptuously fitted up.

I visited the Senate Chamber thrice and heard Blaine and Vance;[44] the house, once, where I heard a confused noise from the floor, and a speaker vociferously demanding order, which calls he emphasized by *coups de baton*. Alexander H. Stevens,[45]

43. The Italian-born Constantino Brumidi (1805–1880) decorated the Capitol with frescoes depicting allegorical subjects and scenes from American history. The painting that Chesnutt mentions was entitled "The Apotheosis of Washington."

44. James G. Blaine (1830–1893), Republican party leader and senator from Maine; Zebulon Baird Vance (1830–1894), Democratic senator from North Carolina from 1879 to 1894.

45. Alexander Hamilton Stephens (1812–1883) was Democratic representative

old and decrepit, still rolls his invalid chair to the front, and talks for his constituency. I was anxious to see Bruce,[46] the Colored Senator, but did not have that pleasure as he was always absent when I visited the Senate Chamber.

All the National Buildings at Wash. are massive and costly structures[.] To get a proper idea of their size and beauty, it would be profitable for the stranger to go the round of the P.O., Pat. O., and other department buildings before visiting the Capitol, since after the full blaze of its splendors, the others look tame in comparison.

I had heard of the extreme difficulty of obtaining Gov. employment at Washington, before I left home. After my arrival in the City I heard still more about it. The places are all, or nearly all, gifts of political favoritism, and without great influence and some cheek, ability amounts to nothing. A man of ability, however, with some friends, and who will stick to the city for several months and worry down his Congressman, may *possibly* succeed. As I had neither time, money, nor inclination for this sort of campaign, I did not engage in it. Before I left the city however, I succeeded in delivering my letter of introduction to Sen. Vance, who then told me what he had answered to my letter of a week before;—that, as far as an office was concerned, there were none to be got; that there were more stenographers in Washington than could obtain employment. My letters to Russell and Ranson[47] I did not attempt to deliver, knowing that it would be useless.

On the first day of my visit I went over to the P. O. Department, and saw George Richardson of Cleveland,[48] who is a Clerk in Auditors office. I went up home with him in the after-

---

to Congress from Georgia from 1873 to 1882. He had been vice president of the Confederate States of America during the Civil War.

46. Born a slave, Blanche Kelso Bruce (1841–1898) served as Republican senator from Mississippi from 1875 to 1881.

47. Daniel Lindsay Russell (1845–1908) was Republican representative from the Wilmington district of North Carolina from 1879 to 1881 and later served as governor of North Carolina. Matt Whitaker Ransom, not Ranson (1826–1904), was the Democratic senator from North Carolina from 1872 to 1893.

48. Like Victoria Richardson, another member of the Cleveland family closely tied to Robert and Cicero Richardson Harris. Chesnutt's sister Lillian later married Garrett Richardson.

noon, and met his wife, and Miss Lina Jean, from Cleveland also, a neice of Mr. Harris's and a former correspondent of the "Educator,"[49] and now a teacher in one of the Pub. Schools of Washington. In the course of my visit I met several old acquaintances, Monroe, Barber, Stuart, Miner, and F. T. Hyman who is also an employee in the P.O.D.

The last Wednesday I was in Washington I visited the Pub. Schools of the city, and found them well graded, and generally having efficient teachers. Most of the young ladies seemed very intelligent and some were very good looking. There are 8 colored school buildings in the City, and there are employed in them more than 100 teachers, not more than 2 or 3 of whom are men. This is a wise arrangement, for if there were any inflammable male timber about, there would be more than one flame in progress, which might interfere with their duties somewhat. On Thursday morning I went out to Howard University with W. Mr. or rather Prof. Shadd,[50] whom I had met the Sunday before, showed me through the buildings. The property of the University is considerable: there are three large buildings; Miner Hall, used for the "Ladies' Dormitory," Clark Hall for the gentlemen, and the Main Building which is occupied by the Chapel, Recitation Rooms, Museum etc. The buildings are grouped on a hill overlooking the city; a very healthy location, removed from the noise and dust, and quite near enough for the conveniences of the city. A street car line runs by the gate, and the mail is carried out twice a day.

The general impression which I recieved of Washington was favorable. It is large, systematically planned, embellished with broad avenues, parks, handsome public and private buildings; the women are good looking—at least very many of them—and the people have that easy and self-possessed bearing which is common to the denizens of a great city.

49. The *Educator,* a monthly illustrated magazine published in Baltimore by the Industrial Department of the Centenary Biblical Institute, billed itself as "a magazine designed to promote the cause of education among the colored population of the United States."

50. Chesnutt almost certainly refers to Furmann J. Shadd, in 1879 principal of the Normal Department of Howard University and later a professor of medicine. A penciled note over the word "Professor" in this journal entry says "Tutor." The Howard University catalog listed Furmann J. Shadd as tutor in mathematics in the academic year 1878–79.

[Added in the upper margin:] I saw the famous "Pinafore"[51] played in Washington. It is an amusing thing, but what freak of fashion gave it such an unexampled popularity?

The unfavorable Ideas which I conceived were more against city life in general, than against life in Washington alone. There is too much noise, too little fresh air. The water from the hydrants is good, but I prefer to draw mine from a well. There are so many people, and so many men of wealth and distinction that a man must be very rich or very distinguished to attract any notice. Colored people have a great many "privileges" which they do not possess further South, but it requires money to enjoy them to any considerable extent. The colored people of Wash. are very extravagant and spend all their earnings, great and small, in a vain attempt to keep up "style" and a high-toned society.—(So I am *told*)—

These are some of the disadvantages of the city. Of course there is more life and activity, more openings for business, more opportunities for mental improvement, music[,] art, science, the drama, can be enjoyed in large cities. I should like to live just far enough away from a large city to avoid the disagreeable things, and near enough to get a taste of its pleasures.

I received a letter from Susan on Wednesday; as I had seen most of the city, and saw little prospect of obtaining employment, in my line—stenography—I determined to leave for Fayetteville on Thursday. I had intended to return by steamer to Norfolk, but after my trunk was packed and my adieux made I discovered that no boat left that day so, I went by rail via Richmond. I arrived at Weldon at 2 'clock Friday morning, got a bed at the hotel, (which cost me a quarter of a dollar per hour,) and waited for the next train.

I rose early Saturday morning, and inquired for the residence of the Goldsboro Mail Agt. I was directed to a house a short distance from the depot, where I found that the Agt who stopped there was not my Uncle Dallas,[52] but a fellow from Wilmington Joe Hasler. He has been running on that Road 10 yrs. and is about as poor as he was when he begun I suppose (as all Gov.

51. Gilbert and Sullivan's *H.M.S. Pinafore* made its American debut in the 1878–79 season and instantly became one of the greatest successes in American theater history.
52. Dallas Chesnutt, Chesnutt's father's brother.

employees are). I went up to breakfast with him, and he offered to get me a free pass to Goldsboro, so that I might go with Dallas part of the way. I accepted his kind offer, for I learned that the schedule of the R & G R.R. was changed, so that I might have to remain in Raleigh Sunday.

I met Dallas and had a talk with him when the train came in. His wife was in Goldsboro and he liked his place very well, since it paid him 50 pr. ct. more than his other position.

It was 9 o'clock P.M. when we arrived at Wil. I stopped at the Jackson House[,] a small restaurant near the wharf, where the accommodation is not the best but, I must do them the justice to say, the charges are very moderate.

At 2 o'clock next day I left by Mr Murchison, Capt. Garrison for Fayetteville, where I arrived Sunday morning. I found them all well, kissed the baby, took a good bath, ate a warm breakfast, and gave myself up to rest from the fatigue of travelling. Lewis and Pa came up during the day. During the week which has elapsed since my return, several thousand people, more or less, have come up to me with beaming eyes and extended hands, and inquired "how I liked my trip to Washington?" This is a sample of the rapidity with which information is disseminated in this small town, and shows either that I am popular, or that these are inquisitive people[.]

Well I am home again, a poorer but a wiser and happier man. This little experiment has taught me; first, that I did not understand Phonography sufficiently well to become an official reporter; secondly, that If I had it was difficult to get a position, on account of the great competition. I also learned that to travel with comfort and to live in a large city requires considerable money, that employment seeking in a strange place, with the best of qualifications, is a weary work; that the advantages of city life can only be fully enjoyed by the wealthy, while the poor feel the full weight of the discomforts. I found that the adage "Distance lends enchantment," etc is as applicable to a city as elsewhere. Absence from home developed in me some of that old failing home sickness, which I had thought my self clear of.

I think however that what I gained was well worth what it cost me. The change of scene, the survey of a large and beautiful city, my visits to Congress, the speeches of great men, actual contact with many things which are nice to read of and to see;

the visits to the Art Gallery, studios, schools, museums etc. and the intercourse with my friends, have enlarged my experience and knowledge of the world; and, by robbing it of some of the stage effects of distance and imagination, have made me better content to remain at home and work faithfully in my present sphere of usefulness. The fatigues of travelling have rendered home comforts more enjoyable.

It is a fault of youth, and of myself in particular, to want to walk before having learned to crawl. These premature efforts are usually attended with many falls and painful bruises, and finally, after the loss of some valuable time result in a return to the good oldfashioned and laborious process of crawling. I am home again. I shall follow my inclinations during the summer and devote myself to study. I have formed a general plan—one hour daily to Latin, one to German and one to French, and one to literary composition. I shall continue to practice short-hand. An hours work in the Garden, miscellaneous reading and "tending the baby" will occupy the remainder of my time. In this manner I expect to pass a very pleasant summer.

I shall hereafter devote myself to my studies and profession. By industry and economy I shall raise myself still higher in the estimation of my fellow-citizens, and with a permanent situation and an increased salary I hope to be somewhat independent in five or ten years. I have determined, however, to relinquish the unprofitable and dangerous occupation of "aerial architect." So that I cannot say positively what I want or expect to do for any period more than 6 mos. in the future, which is the limit I have allowed to my active imagination.

Christmas, 1879. [53]

> The bells are ringing merrily,
> The fires are blazing cheerily;
> And throughout the land, in chorus grand,
> Ten thousand voices ~~are lifted~~ raise on high,
> ~~In~~ Their praise of Him who came to die,
> > For sinful man.

53. An expansion of the poem begun at Christmas 1878; see p. 102.

The old year, in her maturity,
Hath put on a mantle of purity;
As though the benediction given,
By the white-robed choir of heaven
The old year, moribund, had shriven
From her taint of earthly leaven.
Shrouded in her robe of white,
With glittering fringe of ice bedight,
~~Ready~~ With eyes upturned and claspèd hands
Ready to depart she stands,
And only waits to celebrate
The ineffable morn, when Christ was born.

In every corner of our Christian land,
In humble chapel and cathedral grand
In stately mansion where the rich reside
In lowlier dwellings where the poor abide;
With prayer and sermon and with song of praise,
And hymns unspoken which the humble raise
(Anthems unheard, indeed, by mortal ear,
But heard in Heaven in accents loud and clear
For there the atmosphere is so refined,
So keen the senses of the angelic kind,
That thought transmitted is and is as clearly heard
As to our mortal ear the spoken word)

Yet not alone in prayer and solemn praise
—We celebrate the day in lighter ways,
And at this festive season of the year,
We load our tables with the best of cheer,
That not in words alone our joy we show,
But in good deeds, that all the world may know.
We clothe the naked, feed the poor,
And turn none empty-handed from our door.

Around our fires friend meets, in love, with friend;
Care is laid by, and thoughtful brows unbend;
The pale cheek brightens with unwonted glow;
Feuds are forgot, and kindly feelings grow,
Children are happy in their careless play;
Maidens are smiling, and their lovers gay,

The bells are singing merrily,
The fires are blazing cheerily;
And throughout the land, in chorus grand,
Ten thousand voices are lifted high,
In praise of Him who came to die
      For sinful man.

                              C. W. C.

Mar 11th 1880. My Journal is a sort of mental Phonograph, into which I speak my thoughts by means of the pen; and at any future time I can recall them by simply opening the book. If it could copy my thoughts without the aid or intervention of the pen, it would contain a great many more than it does; for, with school and church, with shorthand and music, with correspondence and general reading, my time is so fully occupied that I seldom write in my Journal. I frequently have a bright thought flash, like a meteor through my mind—the plan of a story which I wish to write in the future; —a striking character, which I think would figure well in a novel; —a poetic fancy; —a new invention in mechanics; but most of them disappear like meteors, after flashing across my mind, though I may hope they will reappear at some future time.

I have thought, during the great revival which is going on, that a collection of the ballads or hymns which the colored people sing with such fervor, might be acceptable, if only as a curiosity to people, literary people, at the North.[54] Though these songs are not of much merit as literary compositions, they have certain elements of originality which make them interesting to a student of literature, who can trace, in a crude and unpolished performance, more of the natural ability or character of the writer than in the more correct production of a cultivated mind. Burns and Bunyan[55] rank, in literature, far

54. This music was first recorded in print for a northern audience in William Francis Allen, Charles Packard Ware, and Lucy McKim Garrison, *Slave Songs of the United States* (ca. 1867). It was further popularized by J. B. T. Marsh, *The Story of the Jubilee Singers; with Their Songs*, which went through several editions in the 1870s.
55. The Scottish poet Robert Burns and the Nonconformist Protestant English writer and preacher John Bunyan (1628–1688) lend the authority of tradition, here, to Chesnutt's first recorded reflection on the possibility of a vernacular literature.

above many inferior authors who could manufacture polished Alexandrines and heroic couplets, and who paid far more attention to the external graces of style. Their originality lay in their simplicity and in that force which accompanies simplicity [revised to: received an additional charm from their simplicity of style]. The thunderbolt inspires us with awe; while the same force, confined in a battery, and transmitted along the wires of the telegraph, only excites our admiration. These ballads, like Sankey's[56] most popular songs, take some figurative subject, as "The Life-boat," the "Gospel Train," "The Old Ship of Zion," and carries out the ~~simile~~ metaphor to a considerable extent. The verse is generally the merest doggerel, but the ideas are often good. The tunes are especially adapted to congregational singing; the verse is usually sung in a sort of recitative, or a very simple melody, like Sankey's "I am so glad that my father in Heaven["]; and the best part of the music comes in the chorus. The leader, accompanied by those who have ballads, or know the words, sings the verse, when the whole congregation joins in the Chorus. The words are generally very distinctly sung, and the time is perfect. The most of the ballads are sung in quick time, quite different from the slow tiresome drag with which the ordinary hymn-tunes are sung. The good time is due partly to the simple perfect rhythm of the tunes, and partly to the habit of keeping time with the feet or the upper part of the body during the singing.

I have thought of publishing some of these ballads. I shall at any rate make a collection of them, words and music, and if I, at any time, find it profitable, I will have them published, separately or *en masse*. Elder Davis[57] has kindly furnished me with the words for several, and the music I myself must write.

The revival has never been equalled, either in duration or results, by any which has preceded it in this place. 104 per-

---

56. Ira David Sankey (1840–1908), the white musician who collaborated with the evangelist Dwight L. Moody to produce the popular hymns gathered in *Gospel Hymns*. The spirituals Chesnutt goes on to mention had been collected in *The Story of the Jubilee Singers; with Their Songs,* already in its seventh edition in 1877.

57. J. W. Davis, the minister of the A.M.E. Zion church in Fayetteville in the early 1880s.

sons have joined the church[,][58] 400 have professed religion; the barrooms have been nearly depopulated, for the revival has reached some of the most confirmed evil-doers. In addition to this, the minister has raised a debt of $100 due on the parsonage; has bought an organ costing $130; has bought a clock, $10; and has raised his own salary, $125 for three months! He is an energetic man. He has a queer way of mixing up religion and money, and as he is an uneducated man, his personal peculiarities are very prominent. I was amused at his sermon, or rather at certain passages in his sermon yesterday (Tuesday) night. In speaking of The Prodigal Son, he said that "His father thought he would be comforted in his old age by reading some great speech of his son in the 'Congressional Globe'["], and he also made some reference to the "State Penitentiary," in connection with the prodigal son!

March 14th. I have thought of a new invention, a contrivance, to be attached to reed organs, by means of which the position of the reeds may be shifted, so as to enable the performer to play in any key without shifting the position of his hands on the key-board. The music could all then be written in the key of C, and the learner would be spared the labor of learning the eight or ten transpositions in common use[.] Whether my invention would be of any positive advantage to musical science I cannot say. It might, by simplifying the science, bring it within the reach of many who are now kept from it on account of the labor and expense required to master it. I will think further on it.

Mr. Harris *is* very sick, and I do not notice any improvement in his condition. I sincerely hope that he will recover, but fear lest he may not. I understand that some of his *friends* have been making calculations about the future management of the Normal School, in case of Mr. H's death; but he is not dead yet, and even if he should, I am afraid his friends' hopes will be dashed.[59]

58. The number of people who joined the church is not fully legible and may be 704; 104 seems more likely because not all those who professed religion during a revival would have been admitted to church membership.
59. Harris eventually died on October 24, 1880.

I find it quite different to sit on the platform, from what it was to sit in the recitation-room and hear my classes only.

The following lines are part of a poem which I commenced writing some time ago, and which I still contemplate finishing. It is founded on the legend of "The Devil's Footprint"

"A band of gallant youth and maidens gay
Drove out of town one pleasant summer day,
A fishing party and on pleasure bent;
So to a stream some miles away they went,
Famous for trout, and perch of wondrous size,
Among the few in sporting matters wise;
Whose shady banks would form a cool retreat
From city dust and sultry summer heat.

The dewy freshness of the early morn,
The song of birds, the fields of waving corn;
All the bright smiles which nature scatters round,
And clothes with robes of pleasant sight and sound,
Gladdened their hearts, which overflowed with song
And merry laughter, all the road along.["]

to be continued

Mar 16th. Judge Tourgee has sold the "Fool's Errand," I understand, for $20,000.[60] I suppose he had already received a large royalty on the sale of the first few editions. The work has gained an astonishing degree of popularity, and is to be translated into the French.

Now, Judge Tourgee's book is about the south,—the manners, customs, modes of thought, etc., which are prevalent in this section of the country. Judge Tourgee is a Northern man, who has lived at the South since the war, until recently. He knows a great

60. After the Civil War Ohioan Albion W. Tourgée settled in North Carolina, where he became the leader of a political faction advocating Negro suffrage and the rights of lower-class whites *and* blacks against wealth and privilege. With the rise during Radical Reconstruction of a North Carolina Republican party supported by black votes, Tourgée became a superior court judge. After the defeat of Radical Reconstruction Tourgée came to see his struggle to establish an egalitarian society in North Carolina as hopeless. In 1879 he returned to Ohio and wrote his insider's history of Reconstruction in fictional form. His novel *A Fool's Errand* remained a best-seller throughout the 1880s.

deal about the politics, history, and laws of the South. He is a close observer of men and things, and has exercised this faculty of observation upon the character of the Southern people. Nearly all his stories are more or less about colored people, and this very feature is one source of their popularity. There is something romantic, to the Northern mind, about the southern negro, as commonplace and vulgar as he seems to us who come in contact with him every day. And there is a romantic side to the history of this people. Men are always more ready to extend their sympathy to those at a distance, than to the suffering ones in their midst. And the north, their eyes not blinded by the dirt and the hazy moral and social atmosphere which surrounds the average negro in the south, their interest not blunted by familiarity with the state of affairs in the south, or prejudiced by a love of "our institutions"—sees the south as it is; or is ever eager for something which will show it in a correct light. They see in the Colored people a race, but recently emancipated from a cruel bondage; struggling for education, for a higher social and moral life, against wealth, intelligence, and race prejudice, which are all united to keep them down. And they hear the cry of the oppressed and struggling ones, and extend a hand to help them; they lend a willing ear to all that is spoken or written concerning their character, habits, etc. And if Judge Tourgee, with his necessarily limited intercourse with colored people, and with his limited stay in the South, can write such interesting descriptions, such vivid pictures of Southern life and character as to make himself rich and famous, why could not a colored man, who has lived among colored people all his life; who is familiar with their habits, their ruling passions, their prejudices; their whole moral and social condition; their public and private ambitions; their religious tendencies and habits;—why could not a colored man who knew all this, and who, besides, had possessed such opportunities for observation and conversation with the better class of white men in the south as to understand their modes of thinking; who was familiar with the political history of the country, and especially with all the phases of the slavery question;—why could not such a man, if he possessed the same ability, write a far better book about the South than Judge Tourgee or Mrs. Stowe has written? Answer who can! But the man is yet to make his appearance;

and if I can't be the man I shall be the first to rejoice at his *dèbut* and give God speed! to his work.

I intend to record my impressions of men and things, and such incidents or conversations which take place within my knowledge, with a view to future use in literary work. I shall not record stale negro minstrel jokes, or worn out newspaper squibs on the "man and brother." I shall leave the realm of fiction, where most of this stuff is manufactured, and come down to hard facts. There are many things about the Colored people which are peculiar, to some extent, to them, and which are interesting to any thoughtful observer, and would be doubly interesting to people who know little about them.

The following conversation took place today between Mr. G. Haigh, Bookseller[61] and myself. Mr. Haigh read a paragraph in Harper's Magazine, where a lady requests her servant Bridget in a mild and deprecating tone, to perform some slight service, "if it was not inconvenient."

"That's just the way it is getting to be down here," he says. "You can't get a servant to do hardly anything. It is actually getting so that we are almost afraid to tell a servant to do anything. They haven't got time. They don't like to be ordered about, and I would rather, indeed, I do[,] do a great many things myself rather than ask a servant to do them."

"Well," I remarked, "that is one of the inconveniences that the rich have to suffer, that the poor are not troubled with. They do their own work and have no tyrannical servants to domineer over them. Besides if they don't suit you, dismiss them and get others."

"But then you get in a worse condition than before. They don't work like they used to."

["]Well, you see, that is one of the results of slavery;—not of freedom as you are about to say. It is and has been for many years, the custom in the South, to consider labor dishonorable.

---

61. George H. Haigh (1832–1904) owned a bookstore on the northwest side of Market Square in Fayetteville. He later became owner and editor of the *Fayette-ville Observer,* located in the same building. As the views here recorded indicate, George Haigh was a man of conservative social and racial attitudes who gave Chesnutt a place to read and talk, although he never modified his prejudices. His obituary describes him, no doubt with the tact characteristic of the genre, as "a man of positive convictions."

And now that the slave is free, he naturally takes your view of it and don't want to do much any more than he can help. Besides, your servants are more submissive and easily managed than the white servants in the North."

"Oh, no: they can't be."

"You were accustomed, before the war, to prompt and implicit obedience from your servants; and now that they have not the same incentive, the fear of the lash or the corn-field, they are less submissive, and you feel the difference very keenly."

"It's hard to get honest ones, too. It's a pity their ministers don't preach that too them as one of the fundamental doctrines or grounds of their religion."

"Well, they do. And you —"

"Its hard work to get a servant that wont steal. If you hire a negro woman with a family, you may just make up your mind that you have got to support her family; and it would be economy to employ as many of them as possible. They carry off all the cold victuals; and you have to support their pigs and dogs if they have any. You may have pigs on the lot, and they will nearly starve, while the servants carry off the swill to feed their own. And they are so extrava[ga]nt. You've no idea what a quantity of good victuals they throw into that swill."

"You ought to superintend their work, and see that they do it right."

"You *can't* superintend them. If you look into the kitchen, or venture a mild remark about something connected with the housework, they get mad right away, and tell you by their looks, that they don't want any of your interference."

I laughed at the dismal picture, and he continued to expatiate on the shortcomings of servants. His reference to some wine, drew from me the remark that there was less drunkenness among the colored people of this town than might have been expected.

"Yes," he said, "there is[.]"

"It is due," said I, ["]largely to the influence of Mr. Harris. He has taught his scholars, ever since he came here, total abstinence principles; and I ascribe the temperate habits of the younger colored people almost entirely to his influence."

"Well, that is the only way that you can get at them,—begin when they are young, and train them up to it. I don't drink myself, now—used to when I was younger[.] But, now I think of it, of all the young men who grew up along along with me,—there were a hundred of them I suppose,—three-fourths of them have died—have been killed by liquor, or by something—some disease which could be directly traced to the use of liquor. Some from consumption—contracted by exposure—lying out in the weather; some have been killed in drunken brawls—nearly all of them were killed by liquor." His own brother, a man of uncommon ability—a short-hand writer, a student of languages (linguist), a talented lawyer,—after squandering his property and beggaring his children, died drunk.—froze to death one cold winter's night when he was too drunk to get home, and lay down on the street, where he was found dead next morning.

Mar. 25th. I spoke to Elder Davis last night about the congressman from our district—Russell. I had been informed that Davis possessed considerable influence with Russell, which Davis himself claims. He went on to speak about Russell's peculiarities. He is, according to Davis's statement, a very repulsive looking man, with very rude manners. On one occasion, the sheriff of Bladen, I believe, insulted Russell. Russell immediately brought his gold-headed cane into violent contact with the sheriff's head; and then, walking into the courthouse, remarked to the Judge that "He'd thrashed that sheriff o'his'n, and he wanted to pay for it."

Russell once invited Davis to dinner. Davis remarked to Russel that he ought to join the church.

"Well," said Russell, "ain't I good enough? Didn't I give you one-hundred and ten dollars to build a church?"

"Yes, you did all that; but you are a sinner—you ought to join the church."

A short time after Russel wrote to Davis that he had joined the church—the *Catholic Church*!

I stated my desire to get a position as a stenographer, or clerk—in Washington. Davis thought he could get anything in Russel's power for me; but he wanted me to stay here.

"I am very sorry to say it, but Prof. H.[62] is going to die. I am very sorry, but it is more than likely, and you must take that

62. Robert Harris.

school. We want it and we'll get it. I was thinking of something else for you too. I thought that I would try and get Russel to make this a port of entry, and we want you for Collector of Customs."

Either of these positions would be a lucrative and desirable one, but—my tastes lie in a different direction. Davis said he ~~could get~~ would do anything I wished, but would rather I should stay. "Time alone will tell."

A novel Idea in Preaching.

"Some people," said Elder Davis as he lit his pipe, and put his feet on the mantel, "don't understand my style of preaching. I've got three classes of people to preach to, and I must so arrange my sermons as to suit all three classes. The first class is educated—been to school—know what preaching is. They are in a small minority. The second class is moderately intelligent, but with very little learning. The lowest class is the ignorant, unlettered, naturally stupid ones who can't be reached by anything but excitement and extravagance. These are by far the largest class.

"Now in order, you see, to please 'em all, that you may keep the church together, and get your salary, you must preach to suit them all. So when I preach, I first go at it in regular pulpit style, fling in a trifle of Latin and Greek, divide my discourse into appropriate heads, and for a while read from manuscript. This is for the intelligent class. Then I come down a little, and preach for a while in colloquial style—don't pay quite so much regard to grammar, don't stick quite so close to my text—only use a big word now and then, as a sort of puzzle you know—keep up my dignity. This is for the second class.

"Now comes the tug of war! The last class must be reached. I shut up the Bible; rumple up my hair; shove up my coat-sleeves;—have taken my coat clean off in country churches; I leave the text altogether, and fall back on my imagination! I first go down to the depths of hell and depict all the horrors of dark damnation; the flames, the anguish, the shrieks and groans of the tortured souls. Then I appeal to sinners to look at this that they are coming to. I forget all about grammar, and come down to plain "niggerisms[.]"

"Then leaving hell, I transport the audience to heaven, and

129

paint the glories of that blessed place. I point to the long white robe, the starry crown, the golden slippers. I use up the Revelation and the older prophets who attempted to describe Heaven, and then fall back on my imagination. About this time, the audience being worked up to the right pitch[,] I bring my fist down on the Bible, knock the water pitcher off the pulpit, and by a final burst of extravagance, bring down the house."

The effect is truly dramatic. I saw Davis once jump down from the pulpit and run across the altar. A scene ensued, such as I had never witnessed before, and never wish to see again. The whole house rose as if by magic. I never was in a mad-house, so I won't make the usual comparison; but I can scarcely conceive anything more—frightful, I guess, will do. The mourners writhed and shrieked with more than their usual vigor, while the christians seemed animated by a common impulse, to make all the noise possible. Here two sisters hugged themselves with suffocating energy. Another threw herself back on the benches with a violence that threatened serious injury to her spine. Another tried to shake hands with everyone in the house. Some laughed hysterically; others cried. Some amused themselves by tearing off their clothes; others, less considerate, but more economical, played sad havoc with that of their neighbors' dress. The sinners cried, "Mercy,["] and got down on the floor as low as possible while the Christians shouted "Glory!" and jumped from the floor as high as possible. Davis let it run a while and then [after] a few minutes stopped it. If animal magnetism—personal magnetism—would work the telegraph, Davis' fortune would be made, for he could furnish enough to run the Atlantic Cable.

"But, my dear sir, do you think this has an elevating effect on the people[?] Is it not as much your duty to try to lift them up as it is to please them[?]"

"Do you see that stick on the floor? I can't pick it up without putting my hand down to it. And so it is with the more ignorant class of our people;—you must go down to them before you can bring them up. You must first stir them up, which can only be done by excitement. Then you can work on them to greater advantage. Its like getting in new ground—you must first grub at the soil, break it up, and then you can cultivate it. The experience of a friend of mine will illustrate this point clearly.

Frederick Jones was a young minister in our church, who had attended a theological seminary, and was a very intelligent young man. When he joined the conference, he was sent to a church down at Frogtown. When Sunday came, he marched into the pulpit, clad in a shiny broad-cloth coat, his boots glistening with Mason's Polish blacking, his shirt bosom stiff as a board, a standing collar of the latest cut, and a clerical tie of immaculate whiteness. His face was shaven clean, and his hair parted just far enough from the middle to rebut the charge of affectation. And as he walked slowly up the aisle, diffusing an aroma of musk as he passed, and, gracefully depositing his shining beaver, and began to pull off his kid gloves,—he thought with serene self-complacency—what an impression he was making upon the congregation.

A hymn was sung, and after a short and somewhat formal address to the Deity, our hero arranged his manuscript, and launched out into a regular doctrinal sermon, which he finished in 25 minutes, by the gold repeater which he so unconsciously took out and glanced at from time to time.

During this time the congregation sat perfectly still. Not a single amen—not a solitary assenting nod of the head marred the perfect propriety which prevailed. It is true that a part of the audience went to sleep, and the faces of a great many others wore a rather disappointed look; but our hero did not notice that.

During the sermon, a rather disreputable-looking old negro, —knock-kneed, unshaven; with a coat out at the elbows, and a pair of old shoes, run down at the heel and run up at the toes, from which the toes of the wearer looked out,—came up the aisle and entered the pulpit; of course the preacher said nothing, but he thought to himself, "I am the Pastor here for this year, and I'll let no such an object as this occupy *my* pulpit." At the close of the sermon he announced that there would be preaching there next Sunday at the usual hour. At this point, an old grey-headed nigger, sitting near the pulpit, got up and said:

"We ain't had no preach dis' mornin' yit. We want brudder Sam to preach for us.["]— "Yes, yes;" came from all parts of the house, "we wants Brudder Sam to preach for us."

The young minister turned to the old darkey who sat behind him, and said:

"Are you a minister?"

"Don't I look like one?"

If Frederick had spoken his mind he would have said "no" at once. But he was a very prudent youth, so he simply said: "Say something to them; they don't seem to be satisfied."

Brudder Sam got up, limped across the pulpit once or twice, and smote the Bible with his fist.

"Amen! Amen!" cried the congregation. He ran across again, a little more rapidly, and then, picking up the bible he brought it down on the pulpit desk with a force that shook the house[.] "*A* men! A men!" cried the congregation again; and Brudder Sam began by remarking that, "Dese fellers comes out heah wid dere starched shirts, and dey' beaver hats, and dere kid gloves, but dey don't know nuffin b[o]ut 'ligion.["]

"Dat's so! Amen! No, dey don't!["] said the congregation; and Brudder Sam went on in a sing-song style, interspersed with frequent groans, and hoarse drawings-in of the breath, and toward the latter part with cries of glory &c,—for an hour and a half, when the congregation was dismissed.

"Fred Jones was a wise youth. He had entered the ministry. He had spent several years of study in preparing for it, and this was the material he had to work upon. He laid his beaver on the shelf and bought a wool hat for half-a-dollar. He got a pair of brogan shoes which he did [illegible word] for six months at a time, and wore his rustiest coat. He left off collars altogether, and wore no more starched shirts; and at the next service, and for many succeeding ones, tried to imitate old Brudder Sam as closely as possible. It was a great sacrifice to the elegant Fred Jones, but he had an object in view. By going down to the people he gained their confidence; and, little by little, has got them up to such a pitch of enlightenment that he can wear his standing collar and kid gloves with impunity, and the people are indignant if a shabbily dressed preacher enters the pulpit."

Mar. 29th. I paid another visit to the learned and eloquent divine whose conversation I last recorded, and I still find him an excellent subject of study. "The proper study of mankind is man";[63] and, while a power of description,—a pen which can point out in glowing language, and reproduce to the mental view of the reader the beauties of nature—golden sunsets, gorgeous scenery[,] purling streams, sparkling cataracts, green fields and bright flowers—is a valuable possession for an author; yet the power to understand human nature, to depict the passions of the human heart,—its loves, its hates; its joys, its sorrows; its ambitions, its disappointments; its strivings after the infinite,— toward a higher life, and the inevitable opposition which it finds in [the] "house of clay," which binds it down to earth,—*this* is a far more valuable accomplishment, and to master it requires a correspondingly larger amount of observation and study.

My friend is a politician. According to his statement he has been initiated into the hidden mysteries of the profession, I may call it; he has walked in the penetralia, and rendered great assistance to Russel in the last campaign. Russel is grateful, or at any rate wise, (for I suppose he wants to run again), and has written to Davis to recommend to him a suitable person to be made Collector of Customs, in case Fayetteville should, as the result of a bill now pending, be made an inland Port of Entry. I recommended, with due filial regard, *paterfamilias,* and Davis says he will consider it. He thinks and says he can get anything from Russell, that is in that astute politician's power; which heaven grant! for I want a position as stenographer at the National Capital. My learned friend thinks they want me here, but agrees to get me the place—he means to try—if I will provide him with an organist for his church, by next summer.

Mr. D's two principles of action, which he expresses in terse and forcible language are: "Think for yourself"; "If you want a thing, you must fight for it." And very good principles they are. In the turmoil of life, the fevered struggle for wealth, for power, for preeminence; and man must *work* and "fight", as the Rev. Mr. Davis bellicosely expresses it, "for what he gets." And the quality of self-reliance is of the first importance, for, if a man can think *well*, it is always best to "think for himself."

63. A famous line from Alexander Pope's "An Essay on Man."

March 30th. It is now my Easter Vacation, and I have plenty of time to write, and plenty of things to write about; the greatest trouble I experience about writing is to get at it.

A few days ago, I was talking to Mr. Haigh[64] about Mr. Harris's health. The conversation then turned on his family; and finally on the colored families who left Fayetteville before the war—in the fifties.

"Those," said he, "were our best colored people. It was a loss to the town when they left[.]"

"Yes, but they couldn't live here. Things were getting too warm for them. You had taken away their suffrage; the laws were becoming more and more severe toward free colored people; and they felt that their only safety lay in emigration to a freer clime. They didn't know how soon they themselves would be made slaves. They had been deprived of every safe-guard of liberty. If one were smitten in the face by a cowardly ruffian, he could not retaliate. He could be swindled of his property, defrauded of his earnings, and could not testify in court of law to the justice of his cause. With such a gloomy prospect is it strange that he should leave.[?] As for my part I can't see how intelligent colored people can live in the South even now." —And I went on to state my reasons why;—the existing prejudice—the impossibility of a rise in the social scale, etc.

Mr. H. thought that these grades of society were the best preservatives of society.

I referred to the prosperous north;—its productions, in art, science, literature; its thrift. I grew rather warm and I am afraid, slightly offended my interlocutor, for he said, he thought that this fretting about one's condition was fighting against God—God placed men as they are. I floored him with the question "Would you consider a slave as fighting against the will of God if he sought his freedom"? He acknowledged that these thoughts were perfectly natural; but asserted that the condition of things would never be different, for the line must be drawn somewhere, and the best plan is to draw it where it is. He spoke with dread of the state of affairs if the social barriers were broken down. I replied that society even in this case, would regulate itself. I asked if they were troubled much with

64. George Haigh, the Fayetteville bookseller.

poor whites at St. John's. He replied in the negative. I argued that the ignorant do not feel at home among the intelligent, and would therefore shun their company, as they do already. But he said things "never, never, never would be changed," and that the only way for a man who doesn't like it to do, is to go away where things are different.

It is strange what fancies sick folks have. Sickness weakens the hold of body upon the mind, and like the horse whose tether is lengthened, it plays wild freaks, and indulges in many extravagancies. Mr. Harris has been taking some medicine of a very pungent and disagreeable taste, and he imagines that everything he eats or drinks tastes of that medicine.

May 8. Mr. Harris is still in a critical condition, which I am afraid will never be less critical than it now is. He has almost lost the use of his legs, which are swollen, the effect, he says of a torpid liver. He goes on crutches, and still cherishes the delusion, which a merciful Providence leaves to us as long as we have any life left, that he will get well. I truly hope he may, but it is extremely improbable. I was struck, the other day, when I went to make out the school bills for the month, at his sending in the bills for the extra money paid out during his illness; and also at the manifest concern which he exhibited with regard to his salary, even when he was in great pain. *Es ist sein grösster Hehler.* [65]

When I presented the bills to Mr. Troy,[66] he refused to sign for the extra money, and rather caustically remarked, that we mustn't kill the goose that lays the golden egg.

The last week has been a week of incidents anyway. On Friday before last, at night, I attended the Republican convention at the Market House, and like a fool accepted a nomination for town commissioner, after once declining. The next day my friends remonstrated; Mr. H. spoke of my indiscretion; and Capt. Williams, Powers, and several others contrived to put so

---

65. "It is his greatest secret" (though *Hehler* can carry the further sense of a receiver of stolen goods).
66. W. C. Troy, a white member of the Board of Trustees of the Fayetteville Colored Normal School and a county leader of the Democratic party. Troy was repeatedly elected to the state senate.

"many fleas in my ear" that I sent in my formal withdrawal to the Ch'm'n of the committee, and backed off as gracefully as possible.[67]———

May 29, 1880. Susie has been in Wilmington a month. I got a letter from her Thursday saying she would be up on Friday, but she didn't come.—There are just two courses in life open to me. One is the pursuit of pleasure; the other is mental activity, constant employment of the mind and purpose toward some good end,—culture, mental, or spiritual. Neither my tastes nor habits incline me to seek mere animal enjoyment. And my circumstances, my awkward circumstances are not favorable to a very high development either of mind or morals. But my mind is so constituted that it cannot remain idle. "An idle brain is the devil's workshop," and mine is always active, either with good or evil thoughts. Its activity is sometimes burdensome, and at times I long for some means of escaping from my own thoughts. I hold myself fortunate that my thoughts when left to themselves generally incline to the good; but the Devil is a skillful strategist, and throws his darts from within and without, and be careful as I may, the evil will intrude itself and is not easily driven away.

The coarser forms of vice are so repulsive to my very nature that I am never likely to become a drunkard, or a rake. Such vices are easily shunned. One can treat them as he would an enemy, who should enter his house with the avowed intention of doing injury; that is, take him by the collar and turn him out of doors. But these subtler forms of moral evil, which are more intellectual than physical; that cynicism which is bred in the minds of the young when they first begin to see life as it is;

67. Chesnutt's father had served as county commissioner and justice of the peace for Cumberland County in the years of Republican ascendancy. The obscure but obviously humiliating episode that Chesnutt records here reflects the changed prospects for black officeholding after the Republicans' loss of power in the mid-1870s and, apparently, the efforts of the colored normal school's white supporters to depoliticize the school, to separate black educational leadership from more general public power. Mr. H is presumably Robert Harris. Captain Williams is J. D. Williams, president of the Fayetteville Bank and another trustee of the colored normal school. Powers is E. P. Powers, a Fayetteville merchant active in civic affairs.

that distrust of religion; that disbelief in virtue; that disposition to look on the dark side of the world and of humanity; and then those seductive forms in which vice presents itself to the mind as real pleasure;—these forms of evil are like the convivial friend whom we welcome at our table; who amuses us with his sallies of wit and mirth; and though we are conscious that he is exercising an evil influence on our characters, yet we cannot summon the resolution to break off from this fascinating companionship, all the more dangerous because of this same fascination.

I do not know whether it is a sign of a strong or a weak mind, or whether there are many other people similarly affected, but my mind is a sort of mental barometer. In fair weather my spirits are light, I look on everything from a pleasant point of view, and if life doesn't look exactly like a garden of roses it seems to have fewer thorns than I had thought. But let a rainy day set in, and down goes the mental mercury, and my thoughts, sometimes imperceptibly, and sometimes in spite of my utmost efforts, gravitate toward the gloomy and disagreeable.

Now I am inclined to think that this tendency is the result of idleness, aided perhaps by a slight natural tinge of melancholy. I do not mean to say that I am ever, or at least often completely idle. By no means. What I mean by idleness is the want of some healthy *compulsory* occupation for the mind. My profession requires of me about six hours out of the twenty-four; I sleep about eight hours, and the other ten are to be provided for. And it [is] almost as arduous a task to keep busy as it is for a city editor to supply forty columns of matter for a newspaper every day in the week. If one had society, recreation or amusement of any kind it would be easier; but in this supernaturally dull and prosaic town one is almost entirely self-dependent for companionship; and the continual reaction of the thoughts upon themselves, the "iterum iterumque"[68] of the same set of opinions tends to contract the mental vision and to guide it in one continual round from which it is as difficult to escape as for a planet to leave its orbit. A harmonious, healthy mental development requires the friction of mind upon mind. If men never argued, they could never perceive those weak places in their

68. Repetition, over and over again.

own opinions, which their adversaries are so quick to see and animadvert upon. Reading stores the mind with knowledge—"maketh the full man;" writing classifies and arranges the results of the reading; but only debate, argument, interchange and criticism of opinion can give one that skill and judgement which is necessary to select the valuable and reject the worthless. This is one great advantage derived from our literary society, our clubs social and political; it is one of the most valuable features of our system of government. We have the right, and the intelligence to exercise it, of discussing the laws and the laws makers. Every one of our town-meetings, every political canvass, is a school in which the American citizen, however humble, can cultivate self-reliance, judgement, and can prepare himself to exercise those political rights with wisdom. But it is useless to sigh for the unattainable. A child may cry for the moon, but a wise man will accept the inevitable, and, if he cannot get what he would "like" to have, is content to wait for it and in the meantime to supply its place as nearly as possible with some less valuable but more accessible material. Books may partially supply the want of conversation. To read to the best advantage I would suggest the following plan:—When you wish to study a subject, a character in history, for instance, take up a book which treats of the subject, read it carefully, then if you can find it, take a book which looks at the subject in a different light, and as you read compare the opinions of the two writers; take the historical facts of the case, about which there can be no dispute, and putting them all together, come to some conclusion. I think every man should have opinions of his own,—not necessarily different from those of others,—(for there is no subject which would admit of such a diversity of opinion)—but some decided opinion on every subject which is clear enough to admit of it. A man might well hesitate to come to a decision on the question whether the planets are inhabited; but there is surely no man who can not after study and reflection, form an opinion as to whether Napoleon was a statesman and a philanthropist, or only a politician and a soldier—to say the least.

But I have almost lost my subject. "An idle brain is the Devil's workshop," and I was discussing some plan to keep my brain employed. If I remain here all summer, as I probably shall, I must arrange some scheme by which I can keep employed pleasantly and profitably during the three months of our vacation. Hitherto I have devoted my time almost entirely to study during the vacations; but this Summer I must make some provision for exercise of the body as well as of the mind. And as I want to write, why I will draw on my account with the Bank of Memory and Imagination and Experience and try to utilize some of the knowledge of books, men, and things, which I have spent several years in acquiring. I will try to secure teachers for my favorite studies, and this will be an incentive to greater exertion. I will ride; I will buy borrow or hire a boat, and emulate old Izaak Walton[69] in the gentle art of angling; I will rent a piano, subscribe to several papers and magazines, and between them all I think I can ~~kill time to advantage~~ pass the time pleasantly and profitably. I would take music-pupils, but I am afraid of my "bete noir" who would be the first one.

I think I must write a book. I am almost afraid to undertake a book so early and with so little experience in composition. But it has been my cherished dream, and I feel an influence that I cannot resist calling me to the task. Besides, I do not know but I am as well prepared as some other successful writers. A fair knowledge of the classics, a speaking acquaintance with the modern languages, an intimate friendship with literature, etc.; seven years experience in the school room, two years of married life, and a habit of studying character have I think, left me not entirely unprepared to write even a book. Fifteen years of life in the South, in one of the most eventful eras of its history; among a people whose life is rich in the elements of romance; under conditions calculated to stir one's soul to the very depths;—I think there is here a fund of experience, a supply of material, which a skillful pers[on] could work up with tremendous effect. Besides, If I do write, I shall write for a purpose, a high, holy purpose, and this will inspire me to greater effort. The object of my writings would be not so much the elevation of the colored people as the elevation of the whites,—for I consider the unjust spirit of caste which is so insidious as to pervade a whole nation, and so powerful as to subject a whole race and all connected with it to scorn and social ostracism—I consider this a barrier

69. Izaak Walton (1593–1683), best known for *The Compleat Angler,* a discourse on fishing as a meditative sport.

to the moral progress of the American people; and I would be one of the first to head a determined, organized crusade against it. Not a fierce indiscriminate onslaught; not an appeal to force, for this is something that force can but slightly affect; but a moral revolution which must be brought about in a different manner. The Abolition[ist]s stirred up public opinion in behalf of the slave, by appealing in trumpet tones to those principles of justice and humanity which were only lying dormant in the northern heart. The iron hand of power set the slave free from personal bondage, and by admitting him to all the rights of citizenship—the ballot, education—is fast freeing him from the greater bondage of ignorance. But the subtle almost indefinable feeling of repulsion toward the negro, which is common to most Americans—and easily enough accounted for—, cannot be stormed and taken by assault; the garrison will not capitulate: so their position must be mined, and we will find ourselves in their midst before they think it.

This work is of a twofold character. The negro's part is to prepare himself for social recognition and equality; and it is the province of literature to open the way for him to get it— to accustom the public mind to the idea; and by while amusing them to ~~familiarize~~ lead them on imperceptibly, unconsciously step by step to the desired state of feeling. If I can do anything to further this work, and can see any likelihood of obtaining success in it, I would gladly devote my life to the work.

June 25th. Our school closed on Thursday morning. Our Exhibition was held on Wednesday afternoon, and was quite a success. I have heard no expression of dissatisfaction from anyone who attended, and, a presumptive proof that the services were not uninteresting, very few indeed of the audience left during the exercises, though the programme occupied upwards of three hours. Mr Bryan, Editor of the Examiner, and Mr. Cobb, were there.[70] We had invited about fifteen of the principal citizens, but only these two deigned to acknowledge our courtesy by their presence. Well! the State paid for the paper and postage.

70. R. K. Bryan was the editor of the *Fayetteville Examiner*, a newspaper begun in April 1880. The paper closed in February 1883, when it was replaced by the reborn *Fayetteville Observer*. Mr. Cobb is the Reverend S. B. Cobb, listed as a forty-four-year-old white minister in the 1880 census.

I am reduced to my old state of self-dependence. I have not a very exalted opinion of my own character in some respects, and I would like to have a friend, my equal or superior in attainments, talents and ambition. Solitude is best for study, but one needs conversation, and recitation, discussion to fix what he has learned upon his memory. But alas! I suppose I must

"Take the good the Gods provide me"

and resigning myself to the inevitable, cease to long for what is beyond my reach.

I expected, quite confidently, to take private instruction in French and German from Mr. Neufeld, the German teacher,[71] and I had not the slightest doubt that I should be able to take Greek from Mr. Cobb, but

"Mann denkt; Gott lenkt;"[72]

Professor Neufeld's time is so fully occupied that at present he can not possibly take another pupil. He says there have been some objections made on the part of some of his patrons, to his taking a colored pupil. He says however, that nothing of that kind would influence him at all, as he is sufficiently independent to lose 20 scholars if necessary, without experiencing any inconvenience. He lent me a german Reader, and has promised to consider my request still further.

I must take my Journal for my confidant and write in it things that I cannot well tell to other people. "A prop[h]et is not without honor save in his own country and among his own people", and I get a great deal more of encouragement from others than from home folks. The reason I suppose is that home folks cannot appreciate my ~~sentiments~~ talents, cannot understand my studies, nor enter into my feelings. (My Journal will not condemn me for egotism.) My nearest ones in some respect are

71. Emil Neufeld, twenty-five years old in 1880, was a recent immigrant from Germany. (Chesnutt's journal later identifies him as Jewish.) The *Examiner* of April 22, 1880, reports that he has just been appointed the first instructor in German in the Fayetteville white graded school. It also runs this notice: "Mr. Emil Neufeld will commence giving instruction in the German Language on Monday evening next to a class of gentlemen. Those wishing to join the class will please leave their names at Mr. George H. Haigh's Bookstore. Terms $1 per month per pupil." Neufeld is listed as a boarder in the 1880 census. Chesnutt later makes clear that Neufeld had relatives in Fayetteville, presumably his reason for locating there.
72. "Man proposes, God disposes."

farthest away in others. Mr. Neufeld told me yesterday that after I had spoken to him a few days ago, Mr. Kyle[73] who was sitting near, asked him if he intended to give me instruction. Mr. N. answe[re]d that he did not know, and Mr. K advised him not, lest he should lose some of his pupils. Dr. Haigh who made one of the group, took up the cudgels in my defence, and thought the Professor ought to take me if he could. Mr. Harris told me yesterday, that Dr. Haigh mentioned my case to him a few days ago, and said he could sympathize with me, for he know[s] my position, and could imagine my feelings. He recognized my ability and accomplishments, and felt that my lot was a hard one, to be cut off from all intercourse with cultivated society, and from almost every source of improvement.

I am deeply grateful to Dr. Haigh for his appreciation and sympathy. It is a drop of rain in the desert of discouragements by which I am surrounded; and if ever I write a book (?) I will either dedicate it to him, or send him a copy of the first edition. (!) Ahem!

I shall continue my studies as best I can. I have made considerable progress by my unassisted efforts heretofore, and feel that I can make greater now. Mr. Cobb is going away and cannot give me greek, so I have yet to decide whether I will take it or not. I shall read Latin, French, and German; with history, biography, and shorthand thrown in for lighter hours; composition, and music, shall not be forgotten; domestic economy, practically applied to housekeeping will fill up another portion of my time,—and with these friends and companions, silent but eloquent, I shall try to spend the summer pleasantly and with profit.

June 28. Professor Neufeld has consented to give me instruction in French and German—three lessons a week. On Tuesdays and Thursdays from twelve to one, and Saturdays in the morning. I am very happy to have this golden opportunity. I have succeeded tolerably well without any instruction heretofore, but now I will see what I can do with it. I shall pay Nr. Neufeld five dollars per month, and I would willingly pay ten if it were necessary. If I had gone north, as I originally intended, my ex-

73. William E. Kyle, mayor of Fayetteville at this time.

penses would have averaged thirty dollars per month, including my travelling expenses.

I am trying to think of a subject for an essay,—critical or Biographical, and I also want subjects for a series of lectures which I purpose to deliver to the school, or to the literary society next session. I wish to inspire the young men with ambition—honorable ambition, a earnest desire for usefulness and distinction in life; I would point them to the heights of knowledge, and tell them how to attain them; to the temple of fame and how to reach it. It is true they cannot all be lawyers and doctors and divines, but they will all be better men, if they cherish high aspirations. I shall write the lectures or essays and commit them to memory, so that I can deliver them with ease and effect.

I must write a lecture on phonography—the principles of the art; its uses, and the method of learning it.

I shall begin my German lessons on Thursday. I sat down to write but I feel more like reading. My mind has been comparatively idle during the past school session, and consequently there is "an aching void" which books alone can fill, and I shall strenuously exert myself to put something in it during the present summer.

Cash[74]

1877			
Oct 27	By 2 mos. salary		$100.
"	" Amt rec'd for ser. in P.S.		10.
"	To bills paid as follows		
	Due bill for 15.00 —	15.00	
	" " to R.H.	20.00	
	Shoes to H. O.	3.00	
	Washing bills	3.00	
	Board " 2 mo.	20.00	
	Due R. H. adv.	5.00	.66 00
"	Clothes for Louis.		12 00
"	Cash to Gov.		10 00
"	Shirts & U. Th.		4 00
"	Umbrella		1 25

74. In Chesnutt's journal this accounting, done four years before the entries that surround it, is lightly crossed out in pencil.

	"	Tuition & back pay for children	2 05
	"	Books for children	1.65
	"	Dutch & Lewis Haircut	50
	"	Mrs. M. for shirts & buttons	35
Nov. 1	"	Umbrella	1.25
5	"	Handkerchiefs	1.00
6	"	Paper	50
~~Nov. 7~~		~~Music Book~~	2.60
		Sundries indefinite	
Nov. 27		By one month Sal	55.
"		To Board	10.00
"	"	Overcoat per R. H.	20.00
	"	Shoes	6.50
	"	" for Lewis	1.25
	"	Gloves	1.25
	"	cologne, toothpicks [illegible word]	.60
	"	Drawers	2.00
	"	Clothe for waterproof	6.00
	"	thred Buttons & Braid	.90
	"	washing bill	1.50

Failure!

—Ideas: for future use. —

1. The devil's foot-print

2. That burglar—John Drunk under the sofa.

3. A Visit to the Infernal Regions and the influence of modern improvements and inventions in science, upon that venerable institution.

4. The wonderful Conversion of Uncle Isham from Episcopacy to Methodism. Aunt Dinah.

5. Walker Pearce.—

6. Aunt Henrietta Wright—preaching—Organ—prayers—begging.

7. Elder Phillip's—hair—dress—theological opinions—Greek, etc.

8. Love Story.—Beggar Girl—Rich boy—Poor cousin—Rich Lady adopts poor girl. 2.—Rich young lady—Rich young man lover—Poor cousin rival—Rich Y. L. loves poor cousin, but encourages R. Y. M till he makes a declaration, when she dismisses

him with the revelation that she was beggar girl, and that she has not forgot his cruelty—Marries poor Cousin.

9. *July 5. Plan of A Novel* ——

I thought some time ago of a plan for a novel which I may write at some future time. The scene is laid in one of the Southern states. The hero is a young man, octoroon, moderately intelligent. He is studying for the ministry at one of the "Freedman's Colleges["] which have sprung up in the South since the War. He falls in love with the daughter of the President[,] Dr ——, who lives on the College grounds. It happens in this wise.— The young lady is a musician. Our hero possesses some musical talent and the young lady offers to instruct him in music. And the consequence is that while he learns to play the piano, he also learns to love his teacher. She is young and pretty, although a little blue and strong minded; and as her occupation, "teaching niggers[,]" cuts her off from social intercourse with the southern white people, she is thrown upon her own resources and the companionship of the few professors and teachers in the institution. Under the circumstances she finds the company of our hero becoming dangerously pleasant. He awakes to a knowledge of the same fact in relation to her. They both come to the conclusion that it won't do. And so without a word on the subject having passed between them, she sends him word next day that she is indisposed and cannot teach. He[,] after a little calm reflection, writes to say, that his other studies are so engrossing that he thinks it best to discontinue his music at present. She appreciates his motives, and feels grateful.

But "love laughs at obstacles." And after a week of repression and loneliness, Miss —— writes to John to come a[nd] practice a new duet with her. John comes, and plays some Italian air with soft melting music and tender words, and just at the tenderest part he looks up and sees her eyes filled with tears. She catches his look; they see the love in one anothers eyes and in a minute he has her in his arms. He pours out his tale of love and they pass a half hour in elysium; as love grew calmer reason asserted herself, and the question of marriage came up. They discussed the pros and cons, he was all passion, but she was more prudent. Finally they concluded to leave it to the "old man".

Her father was both surprised and angry at the announcement, but, when he thought the matter over his anger moderated or changed to pity for the young folks. Dr ——— was a man of deep feeling and broad sympathys. So he calmly reasoned with the young lady as she had done with herself, and then left it to her to decide. She saw John; and talked with him again and they decided that it was best not.

John left school—went off in the country to teach. But the thoughts of ——— haunted him continually. He was near her once or twice, but with an effort—what an effort—kept away. Finally he went as a missionary to Africa, hoping that time and distance would deaden the pain or efface her image from his heart.

He labors long and faithfully. Finally a few years after, he goes on a visit to a mission station a hundred miles from his— takes a boat rowed by natives. Makes the journey successfully, until near his destination when a storm drives him ashore. He is picked up insensible, and nursed through a serious illness. When he recovers, he recognizes in his nurse his former lover— Miss ——— .

Mutual explanations follow. She had determined to leave America to escape the disagreeable attentions of Professor ———, who by the by is the villain of my story, and ought to have been introduced in the first part.

And then in the wilds of Africa, far, far from civilization, surrounded not by glittering gaslights, gay bridesmaids, ~~and gallant groomsmen,~~ but in the pure air of heaven, under a palm tree, they took upon themselves the vows, which bound them "for better for worse to love and to cherish, till death do us part."

A few years more of missionary life and the wife's health required a change of climate. They sought out a clime free from prejudice and in Italy England or somewhere made friends lived happily, etc etc. ad infinitum.

10. Philosophical or rather medical treatise on the health of dirty children. May it not be accounted for on the hypothesis of "Absorbtion", the Liver Pad medium of introducing medicine into the system?

July 5. I have had several lessons in French and German. I like my teacher very well. He is intelligent, polite, well-educated.

He took the degrees in Philology at his University, and studied Chemistry in Paris, and Anatomy at Oxford England, under Huxley, one of the leaders of the modern school of thought i.e., a scientific infidel. Mr. Neufeld is a relative of Kingsbury and the Brandts.[75] He was elected, he says, to the Lower House of the Reichstag, I suppose, at the age of twenty-two. He has travelled much, having on one occasion accompanied an English Geographical expedition through the U.S. and Mexico. He can teach Latin, Greek, French, Deutsch, and Italian.

He says I have studied German for a time equivalent, in the average scholar, to nine months under a teacher. I have, says he[,] a larger vocabulary, though a poorer accent, than Slocumb, who is a graduate of the University of Göttingen.[76]

The French accent is hard to learn. I am fortunate in getting a teacher who knows it correctly. I am now translating from English to German and French.

Slocumb is translating Arabian Nights. Miss Baker is reading the "Henriade"[77] with poor accent.

I had to undergo the bore this morning of writing four or five pages of paper,—report of the Odd Fellows Celebration. I am not connected with the O. F. at all, and yet I have spent about 3 hours of my valuable time in playing the organ and writing the report for them.

Wednesday July 7. "A fellow feeling makes us wondrous kind." The people here, some of them at any rate, are prejudiced to Neufeld because he is a foreigner and a Jew.[78] J. D. Williams,

75. Kingsbury is William Kingsbury, who lived on Adams Street near Mayor Kyle. The Brandts are the family of Simon Brandt, a Fayetteville merchant born in Germany. The census mentions Hattie Brandt as a niece of William Kingsbury living at his house.

76. Albert Haven Slocumb (1837–1915), born in Massachusetts, owned four turpentine distilleries and ran a business in naval stores. After graduating from Amherst College he studied for several years first in Leipsig, then in Athens, making him one of the best educated men in Chesnutt's town. He settled in Fayetteville in 1866 and became a prominent citizen and a principal representative of liberal sentiment.

77. An epic poem in ten cantos by Voltaire recounting Henry IV's struggle to obtain the throne of France.

78. J. D. Williams, bank president and trustee of Chesnutt's school, has been identified previously. Crawford is probably Rev. Crawford, listed in the 1880 census as a white minister. E. F. Moore, another Fayetteville merchant, became

Crawford, E. F. Moore are some that he mentioned. He says that they are so much prejudiced that he would just like to hurt them real bad once. I wish he would. Some of these purse-proud aristocrats seem to think they own the whole world, and that other people only live because they graciously vouchsafe to permit them.

Graham[79] played Neufeld a sorry trick. Neufeld had some prize-writing, fine German script, executed by some of his young lady pupils. Graham asked him to let him take the writing and send it off, where it would help the Graded school and reflect credit upon the teacher, Neufeld. There was a paragraph about it in the N.Y. Sun to-day and a letter from N.Y. in *Hales Weekly,* or the *"News"* rather, complimenting Mr. Graham on his enterprise in introducing German into his school, and on the proficiency displayed by "Mr. Graham's class in German." My German was very angry at Mr. Grahams unfair course, and taking the paper, he marked the paragraph, and wrote on the margin "You are a fine German Scholar," and dropped it in the mail for Graham.

He says they want him to teach Latin here, and that these fellows know very little latin. They think they are doing wonders when they read Cicero; and Graham, when he gives his class twelve lines in Virgil for the next days lesson, goes home and studies it two hours, and brings the translation to school the next day written out. I didn't think these fellows here were the best scholars in the world, but I had no idea it was so bad as that. The more I learn about them the less I esteem them.

By the by, I wrote a report of the Odd Fellows' celebration today, for which I demanded one dollar. G. C. Scurlock[80] says he will see it paid.

---

president of People's National Bank in the late 1880s.

79. Alexander Graham (1844–1934) took a law degree from Columbia University and briefly practiced as a lawyer, then turned to education, becoming superintendant of schools in Fayetteville in 1878. (He later held the same post in Charlotte.) Later known as "the father of the North Carolina graded school system," he played a crucial role in introducing the grade school to white public education, imitating, for the benefit of white pupils, the graded school for blacks that Robert Harris headed and Chesnutt taught in (see Introduction, 8). He had hired Neufeld as German teacher for the graded school in April 1880.

80. George Scurlock, a black businessman and civic figure who later settled in Washington, D.C.

July 13. John Green[81] has written a book. I have just finished reading a review of it in the Cleveland Herald. The review or resumé rather occupies more than a column. It speaks in very complimentary terms both of the book and the author. The subject is the author's experience in the South. The work is issued anonymously and purports to be written by a "Carpetbagger who was born and bred there." I suppose I must get a copy.

This is one of those ephemeral productions which have sprung up in the wake of the "Fools Errand." This remarkable book has, I suppose, created an appetite for this sort of literature. But the colored man is still in America, and likely to be here for some time to come; and he will never cease to be the object of popular interest and sympathy in the north, as long as he is the object of oppression and prejudice at the South. So I will wait awhile before I publish my book,—wait till I am better prepared to do justice to the subject and to myself.

I will get a copy of Green's Book, and see what it is like. If I were not studying French and German now I would try my hand on something light for the press. I think the N.Y. Witness would nurse me till I acquire some skill and strength. I may be mistaken, but I think some of my verses are at least as good as the average newspaper poetry, which is saying very little for them. I expect the Cleveland Herald would pay me for Southern Correspondence. I have a vast fund of raw material on hand for stories and sketches, and I ought to be able to work some of it up.

I am reading Goethe's "Faust," the masterpiece of German Literature. I was struck by the familiarity and flippancy of Mephistopheles in his conversation with the Lord in the "Prolog im Himmel," but my teacher explained this by saying that Goethe himself was an unbeliever, with little regard for sacred things. The idea in the first part of the story where the Lord gives the devil permission to lead Faust astray is borrowed, adapted, plagiarized, or paraphrased from the same incident in the story of Job, where the Lord gives the devil permission to tempt Job. The subsequent plan of the story however is widely different, and presents few points of similarity; for

81. John Patterson Green (1845–1940), a black North Carolinian who moved to Cleveland and became a successful lawyer and member of the Ohio Gen-

Job maintained his integrity, while Faust fell an easy prey to Mephistopheles. But I must read more before I criticise further.

July 25. When Wash. Anderson was out of his head, he had a certain pressure of the hand which he called the Holy Grip. Any mischievous boy could give W. the grip and be pronounced "all right"; while the good old Christians who didn't know the grip, were denounced as wolves in sheep's clothing[,] reprobates of Hell.

Aug 4. I am getting along finely with my German and French. One or two more lessons will take me through the first book, and then, after a rapid review, I will be ready for the second, which, as far as grammar is concerned, completes the course.

The German language is rich in proverbs, and they are much more frequently employed than in English. I find many of them in "Faust"; they are often the same that we have in English.

> { "Ein Dienst ist wohl des andern werth"
> { "One good turn deserves another"
> > { "Aus den Augen aus dem Sinn"
> > { "Out of sight, out of mind"
> { "Die Kunst ist lang, und kurz is unser Leben"
> { "Art is long and time is fleeting."

I have written some scraps of verse at odd moments, which I will write down and preserve. There [They] are hardly worth keeping; but I can improve them perhaps and bring them up to the standard of the common newspaper poetry, (which is poor). The first, "Ode to the moon," was written about twelve o'clock at night, after a day of work and study,

"To the Moon."

Fair Moon, thy gentle face

Looks down from Space

---

eral Assembly, published a book entitled *Recollections of the Inhabitants, Localities, Superstitions and Kuklux Outrages of the Carolinas. By a "Carpetbagger" Who Was Born and Lived There* in Cleveland in 1880. A cousin of Chesnutt's, in his later book *Fact Stranger Than Fiction: 75 Years of a Busy Life* (1920) Green records that he visited Robert Harris, Chesnutt, and the Fayetteville Colored Normal School in the late 1870s.

And with its pleasant light
    Makes the earth bright,

Vicegerent of the *Sun*—
    That brilliant one
        Whose rule brings with it life
           And care, and strife,—

Thine is a milder sway.
    Thy clear cold ray
        Although with warmth not blest
           Brings with it rest.

Rest from the toil and pain
    Which once again
        When thy brief reign is done
           Comes with the sun.
Oh, that this life of mine
    Could be like thine
        Pure, calm, serenely sweet,
           For heaven meet.

———

I would dry up men's tears
    Dispel their fears
        Teach them the way of love,
           Lead them above.

When I my course had run
    And the bright sun
        Came on the azure field,
           Softly I'd yield;

Happy if I could read
    Some kindly deed
        If but a little one
           That I had done.

    Ode to the Rising Generations.
Sons of America,
On to the battlefield!
There in the thickest fight,
Boldly your axes wield.

Hew down your enemies,
Victory! the battle cry
Break through their serried ranks,
Conquer or die!

Fight against Ignorance;
This is our greatest foe.
She, on the field of death,
Has laid her thousands low.

Fight Superstition;
It is her strong ally:
Fight it with reason calm
Soon it will die.

Cut down the hydra Vice
Crafty and bold is she.
Always be vigilant;
Faithful and valiant be.

And against unjust laws—
Legalized infamy.—
Fight wrong in Church and State;
Show them no sympathy.

Truth is your battle-ax,
Life is your battle-field
God your Commander is,
Justice your shield.

Sons of America—
Ye of the dusky hue;
In the world's conflict be
Faithful and true.

Sept 8. Mr. H[82] says that when a small boy, he was a whig, although his father was a democrat. He thinks his political opinions were influenced by a rhyme which was common in those days;

"Whigs,
Feed on pigs,

82. Again, probably George Haigh.

And ride in gigs.
Democrats,
Eat dead rats
And ride on cats."

and as he always had a eye toward the good things of this world,
he was a whig.

Circus.— Colored party. "Lor' what's dat coming long dere, with
a tail on his head"? *Other colored party.—* ["]Lor' niggah, don'
you know, da's de elephum, he ain't got no tail on his head; dat's
his *snout.*"

Mrs. Buxton[83] would be a bully character to write up. She can
drive a two-horse carriage, can browbeat a stump speaker, write
an essay, make a speech, keep her household in order, and wear
the breeches without any objection on the part of the Judge,
whom she has well in hand.

Feb 24 / 81. If I were Judge Buxton, I would lock "Miss Buck" up.
Her conduct is positively disgraceful. She went up to Raleigh
yesterday and repeated with staples from the Senate Gallery,
the same scene she enacted with Jarvis during the campaign.[84]
The bill to compromise the Fayetteville debt was up and she
kept up a running fire of remarks during the discussion, ques-
tioning the speakers, denying their statements, and just making
a fool of herself. She is almost a candidate for a lunatic asylum.
She'll make a splendid character to write up.

"If mistakes was all haystacks, dey wouldn't be so many po'
hosses."

Henrietta McDonald

---

83. Rebecca Bledsoe Buxton, the wife of Judge Buxton.
84. Judge Buxton had run as the Republican candidate in the North Carolina
gubernatorial election of 1880, losing to the Democrat Thomas J. Jarvis by an
unexpectedly narrow margin.

In looking over this journal, I have come to the conclusion that if I should ever distinguish myself, and some of my descendents or friends should undertake to write my life, unless they were persons of excellent taste and literary judgment, I would go down to posterity as a most conceited fellow. I have written a great deal about myself, more than I would like to read of any authors writings about himself. But as I am writing for myself, and not for posterity, it's nobody's business.

Mr. Barney Watson, one of our students, very green, introduces himself to Miss Jane Taylor after the following manner; "What might be your name, Miss?" "Jane Taylor's my name." "Well Miss Jane Taylor, meet Barney Watson; Mr. Barney Watson, Miss Jane Taylor." "Miss Jane Taylor, I've loved you ever since I first seen you, etc,[."]

Saturday, March 26. I have just finished Thackeray's "Vanity Fair", his first great novel.[85] He had written much previous to its appearance, but with "Vanity Fair["] he made himself a reputation.

Every time I read a good novel, I want to write one. It is the dream of my life—to be an author! It is not so much the *monstrari digito,*[86] though that has something to do with my aspirations. It is not altogether the money. It is a mixture of motives. I want fame; I want money; I want to raise my children in a different rank of life from that I sprang from. In my present vocation, I would never accumulate a competency, with all the economy and prudence, and parsimony in the world. In law or medicine, I would be compelled to wait half a life-time to accomplish anything. But literature pays—the successful. There is a fascination about this calling that draws a scribbler irresistibly toward his doom. He knows that the chance of success is hardly one out of a hundred; but he is foolish enough to believe, or sanguine enough to hope, that he will be the successful one.

I am confident that I can succeed, in some degree, at any rate. It is the only thing I can do without capital, under my

85. William Makepeace Thackeray's *Vanity Fair* was published in 1848. A penciled note after the day and date of this entry says "81" (or 1881).
86. "To be pointed out as a famous person."

present circumstances, except teach. My three month vacation is before me after the lapse of another three, and I shall strike for an entering wedge in the literary world, which I can drive in further afterwards. "Where there's a will etc", and there is certainly a will in this case.

Tom McDonald's Lesson.[87]

When Tom McDonald was a young man, there was a wedding over the river, where he lived, and nearly every body in the neighborhood was invited except Tom. Thinking that they had forgotten him, Tom determined to go anyway, and on the evening of the wedding, presented himself at the door about eight o'clock when the company had nearly all gathered.

"Why its Tom McDonald" said the old man, as he came to the door[,] "come in Tom come in; you ain't invited here, but God knows you're just as welcome as if you was."

The old man's grasp of Tom's hand was so cordial, and as no one was present to hear the part about the invitation, Tom began to feel comparatively easy. But his complacency was soon disturbed[.] The old man led Tom along the passage to the parlor door, and as Tom stepped in, announced him to the company as follows.

"Ladies and gentlemen, this is Tom McDonald. He wasn't invited here, but he's just as welcome 'zef he was."

The girls snickered and the boys grinned; but Tom was a handsome fellow, and the girls were not sorry to see him; and as he was six feet high and every inch a man, the boys didn't think it prudent to make much of a demonstration. It was rather embarrassing, but country folks are not so hyper-refined as town folks, and Tom was not sensitive so he mingled with the crowd and soon forgot all about it to the tune of old Dan Tucker, which was the result of the combined efforts of two darkies on a "chist" in the corner.

About ten o'clock supper was announced. The boys and girls

87. This piece forms the germ of one of Chesnutt's first published stories, "Tom's Warm Welcome," which appeared in the story paper *Family Fiction* in 1886. The text of the published version can be found in Sylvia Lyons Render, ed., *The Short Fiction of Charles Waddell Chesnutt* (Washington, D.C.: Howard University Press, 1974).

paired off and marched in, all except Tom, who was too bashful or else too slow to get a partner. The old man ushered them in, as Tom brought up the rear and entered the dining room, the old man cheerily exclaimed in his usual high-pitched voice: "Come in Tommie, come in; there's plenty to eat. You wasn't invited here, but you're just as welcome as if you was. Don't be bashful; there's plenty for all; and there'll be some left for the niggers."

This was almost too much, but the long table, with its tempting array of chicken and cake, and syllabub; and the two big jugs on the sideboard were too attractive, and poor human nature succumbed to the temptation. The boys & girls snickered worse than before, and Tom felt rather down. As soon as supper was over he felt for his hat and tried to slip off without being seen[;] as he got to the door the old man stepped in from without, and seeing Tom, bade him good bye.

"Goin' Tom? Don't be in a hurry! Must go, eh? Well I'm sorry. You wasn't invited here, but we've enjoyed your company just as much as if you had been."

~~This was the last straw,~~

An unmistakable roar followed the old man's good by, and as Tom rushed away, he swore a deep and solemn vow never to go again where he was not invited.

THIRD JOURNAL,
1 8 8 1 – 1 8 8 2

Jan 3d 1881. As it is customary to make new plans, and form good resolutions for the year at its beginning, I have resolved, among other things, to resume my journal. I may fail to keep this resolution, along with the others, but I shall begin it, at any rate.

I have always found keeping a journal very pleasant, for various reasons, and the same will apply to this one. Cast, as my lot has been, among a people, or in a place whose people do not enter into my trains of thought and who indeed cannot understand or sympathize with them, I find it quite a relief to take them to my confidant, my Journal, who listens patiently as long as I care to talk, never contradicts my statements, and keeps my secrets religiously. My Journal, like my valet (if I had one) will know all my weaknesses, yet will neither betray them, nor presume upon them.

I have been on a "Northern Spree" for nearly a week. The Christmas Holidays are just over, and during the whole time I hadn't a single—well, only one—invitation anywhere. The dullness of the place, combined with my own idleness, led me to draw comparisons between the North and the South which were by no means favorable to the latter. I occupy here a position similar to that of the Mahomet's Coffin. I am neither fish[,] flesh, nor fowl—neither "nigger", poor white, nor "buckrah." [1]

1. The African-derived word *buckrah* was blacks' name for a white man or a person in power. "Po' buckrah," the sense Chesnutt likely intends here, designated poor whites or so-called white trash.

157

Too "stuck-up" for the colored folks, and, of course, not recognized by the whites. Now these things I would imagine I would escape from, in some degree, if I lived in the North. The Colored people would be more intelligent, and the white people less prejudiced; so that if I did not reach *terra firma,* I would at least be in sight of land on either side.

Egotism is a disagreeable fault. I mean to be as egotistical as I please in my Journal. I believe that I am not as vain or conceited as many would be in my place. I have my share of self-consciousness—that morbid sensibility and extreme susceptibility which is called by that name—but I cannot unmake myself. I can keep it down but the "leopard cannot change his spots, or the Ethiopian his skin."

Jan 15. The week is nearly over. Our Examination is well over, the scholars properly classified, and the school in good working order. The Sen. Class begin Physics, which I think is an important study; the Senior and Mid. both take Quackenbos's Composition,[2] which I consider a most necessary study.

Gov. Jarvis's message to the Legislature is very good.[3] He recommends that the Normal School appropriations be increased "if possible," and doesn't specify the am't. He recommends, however, a "small addition[al]" annual appropriation of $1,000 to the State University. $1000 a year would set our school on a pinnacle of prosperity; but I expect it will be long before we get it.

Elder Davis, I think, is getting to the end of his rope. He has been playing fast and loose for some time. His love for liquor, his abuse of the people, his conceit[,] arrogance, and impudence, together with his fondness for the fair sex, and his lax method of conducting financial matters, have borne their legitimate fruit; and when the reaction comes, (and I think it is setting in now,) his fall will be as great as the elevation to which the people raised him when he first came here. Too much power

2. Chesnutt presumably refers to G. P. Quackenbos's *Advanced Course of Composition and Rhetoric,* the text he himself used in 1874, but he may mean Quackenbos's *First Lessons in Composition,* the two hundred thousandth copy of which was issued in 1870.

3. By state law, the Fayetteville Colored Normal School and the University Normal School both received an annual appropriation of $2000. Thomas Jordan Jarvis (1836–1915) served as governor of North Carolina from 1879 to 1885.

and popularity will spoil any man; the people are not competent to judge justly of a man's abilities, and take this extraneous success as a type of the "inner man." Davis has presumed too much on the ignorance of the people, and they are both beginning to find out their mistake.

8 p.m. Cotten[4] called this morning. He tells me that Davis met the Board of Church Trustees last night and blarneyed them so successfully that they withdrew all their charges, and begged his pardon for ever having made them. Davis is a wily villain; he covers his trail so carefully that they cannot prove anything against him. His "rheumatism" accounts for his unsteady gait, his medicine for the smell of whisky of which his clothes and breath are redolent; his neice must have company, and the Rosebuds must meet, so these give him frequent opportunities for enjoying the company of the fair Jane. Well, "murder will out", and Davis will yet be unmasked; it is only a question of time.

I gave up my French and German at the beginning of the year. I cannot afford to pay for it, and I think I have about ~~cleaned~~ used up my teacher. Not that I know a tithe of the German or French that he does; but I have got to the end of my method, and he doesn't seem to know much about oral instruction. As an offset to the loss of the Ger. and Fr., I shall, during the remainder of the session, take a thorough course in History and poetry. I have already read Goldsmith's Rome, Macaulays Life and Letters, and have begun Merivals Rome, which I shall read with the greatest minuteness.[5] I know a great deal, but a great deal of what I know is superficial. I want to be a scholar, and a scholar should be accurate in all he knows.

Macaulay's Life is very interesting. The first volume more so

4. Of the several Cottens in Fayetteville this is probably Wesley Cotten, listed in the 1880 census as a black schoolteacher aged twenty-four.

5. Oliver Goldsmith's *Roman History from the Foundation of the City of Rome, to the Destruction of the Western Empire* was first published in 1769. *Goldsmith's Roman History, Abridged by Himself, for the Use of Schools* had its first American edition in 1795 and was reprinted many times through the nineteenth century. Thomas Babington Macaulay (1800–1859) was a Whig statesman and member of the Supreme Council of India whose works of history and biography were much admired during the Victorian era. *The Life and Letters of Lord Macaulay*, by Macaulay's nephew George Otto Trevelyan, was published in 1876. Chesnutt was likely reading the edition of Charles Merivale's *General History of Rome from the Foundations of the City to the Fall of Augustus* published in Harper and Brothers' Student's Series in 1877.

I think than the second. Perhaps the record of his early college successes, his success in Parliament; his letters breathing a lofty yet honorable ambition, are more interesting to a young man than the history of his declining years. His was a great and glorious career. A life of happiness, surrounded by books which he loved, and relatives who filled the place which nature had formed for his children; successful in college, in Parliament, in literature. I would not wish for a nobler career. If I could earn a tenth part of his fame, or make a tenth part of his money, I would have good cause to be content. Truly as one of his contemporaries said, "He had no cause for discontentment"; he was born under a lucky star.

Jan 21st. I had a conversation with Robert Hill[6] last night, about Southern affairs. He is a very intelligent man, uses good English, and understands what he talks about. He was once a slave, and was badly treated. His argument to the white man who tried to coax him to come over to the Dem. party, and "let them darn Yankees alone," was, "Take away all the laws in our favor that "them darn Yankees" have made, and what would be left?" He believes that the local affairs of the South will be best administered by the property owners, but he is "stalwart Republican" in all national affairs—in all of which we agree.

He related a conversation he had with Jno. McLaughlin—a poor white man, and a clerk in Williams's store.

"Bob," said McLaughlin, "what kind of fellow is this Chesnutt[?"]

"Well, sir, he's a ~~nigger~~ perfect gentleman in every respect; I don't know his superior."

"Why! he's a nigger, ain't he?"

"He's classed with the colored people, but—["]

"Well, what kind of an education has he?"

"He's not a college bred man, but he has been a hard student all his life. You can't ask him a question he cannot answer."

"He's this short-hand writer," musingly.

"Yes, sir."

"Does he think he's as good as a white man[?]"

6. Robert Hill is listed as a thirty-four-year-old black drayman in the 1880 census.

"Every bit of it, sir"; and he might have added, if he had known my opinions, that I would think very meanly of myself if I didn't consider myself better than most of the white men I have met in this vale of tears.

Hill then went to argue about the equality of intelligence and so on, but McL. wound up with this declaration, which embodies the opinion of the South on the "Negro Question".

"Well he's a nigger; and with me a nigger is a nigger, and nothing in the world can make him anything else but a nigger." Which reminds me of the sentiment expressed by an old poor white beggar, who was at the time eating scraps in a colored man's kitchen[:] "Well, for his part, let other people think as they please, he always did like niggers as long as they kept in their place, and he wasn't ashamed to say so either."

I got some new light on the Union Leage.[7] It seems that the League once suspected the whites of a plot to blow up the lodge where the league met, and a keg of powder was found concealed there. They immediately resolved to defend themselves, and the white folks were given to understand that if they had the firearms, the nigger had the torch—a significant ~~threat~~ hint which had the effect desired.

Saturday. Jan 22nd. I have devoted nearly the whole day to answering letters. An hour or so was spent in copying poems for the "Star of Zion,"[8] a very poor paper which I hope my verses will improve somewhat.

> *To Helen*
> Sweet is her name
> Sweeter her face!
> On every feature
>   A charm finds place.
>
>   Smiling, like sunshine,
>   When 'tis fair weather;

7. Union League Clubs were first formed in the North in 1863 to help with soldier relief and the recruiting of volunteers. After the war the Union League developed into a Republican political organization in the South strongly linked to the black vote and black political rights.

8. One of the principal Negro newspapers of North Carolina, the *Star of Zion* was published in Salisbury. It was supported by the A.M.E. Zion church.

Coy as a bluebell,
Hid in the heather.

Her every movement
Is filled with grace;
And love, like a halo,
Shines round her face.

I loved thee, sweet Helen!
When first thy blue eyes,
    Cupid
Like *an army* in ambush
Took my heart by surprise[.]

Can I live without thee?
Thy love is my life;
My dearest ambition
To call thee my wife!

———————

A Fragment
Over the stormy sea,
Leaving my heart with thee,
Taking thy heart with me
In search of wealth for thee
Boldly I rove
Fearing nor wind nor wave,
Breakers and storms I brave,
Live but to be thy slave,
To earn thy love!

Feb. 27 / 81. A week ago yesterday I was in Raleigh, in the interest of the Normal School: I made a good impression up there, and have since been referred to, in the "News"papers and in debate in the Senate, as "Prof. Chesnutt"; and in the Com. on Education as a "scholar and a gentleman". White and Hicks,[9] both colored members from the East, wanted the Nor-

9. Alexander Hicks represented Washington County in the North Carolina House of Representatives in 1881; George H. White was a black lawyer from Bladen County elected to the state legislature in 1881 and later elected to the U.S. Congress. The controversy Chesnutt alludes to was resolved in the summer of 1881 when the legislature authorized four additional colored normal schools

mal School moved to Goldsboro or Newbern, and the teachers appointed by the Legislature. But the Com. supported our
school, and took the wind out of White's and Hicks's sails.

The present Legislature are of quite a liberal turn of mind.
The school bill, which has just passed[,] provides for 12½¢ tax
on the $100, and 37½¢ on the poll; in case this is insufficient
to run the schools four months[,] a special tax is to be levied in
each co.

March 12, 1881. Saturday. I have just finished Merivale's General
History of Rome. I like it very much. It is calm and judicial in
tone, and so far as my knowledge of history will allow me to say,
perfectly impartial. He rather leans toward the orator Cicero,
and does not dwell on his vanity and cowardice as much as other
writers. His account of the civil wars is very full, as indeed it
should be, for that is the most interesting or the most prominent period of Roman History. His account of the last two or
three centuries of the Empire is somewhat hurried, which the
size of the book probably accounts for.

I shall now take up "Greeley's American Conflict",[10] and read
it in connection with such other works on American History as I
can procure. I shall pay special attention to the political history,
and the governmental policy.

To Shakspeare
Illustrious poet! thine the pen,
Which paints the minds and heart of men;
Thy lines shall future ages trace,
The Homer of the Saxon race!

Monday, March 14. I have concluded to take [a] week's rest before beginning the American Conflict. I do not mean absolute
rest,—variety, or change would perhaps be the better word. I
shall spend a good part of it in making out the report which
has been requested from me by the Bureau of Education. My

at New Bern, Plymouth, Franklinton, and Salisbury. These schools received
only one quarter of the subsidy provided for the Fayetteville school.
10. Horace Greeley's history of the Civil War, *The American Conflict,* was first
published in 1864, then completed with a second volume in 1867. It continued
to be one of the great best-sellers of the post–Civil War decades, marketed—
like the later *Personal Memoirs of U. S. Grant*—through subscription publishing.

music-pupils will take up four hours; and if I have any leisure I will write in my journal, or work on my Lecture on the Negro as a Soldier, which ought to have been completed long ago.

I was reading Goethe Saturday, and thought the "Prison Scene" in Faust the most touching thing I ever read. I notice many little passages like Tennyson.

"Die Kunst ist lang und kurz ist unser Leben."

"Art is long, and time is fleeting."

and several others. But that is nothing strange. Two men of the nineteenth century, both educated according to the conventional mode, cannot but have many thoughts in common, though they are perfectly original so far as the individual is concerned.[11]

March 17, Thursday. I have skimmed "The Negro in the Rebellion," by Dr. Brown, and it only strengthens me in my opinion, that the Negro is yet to become known who can write a good book. Dr. Brown's books are mere compilations, and, as Thos. Jefferson says of Phillis Wheatley[']s poems, "beneath the dignity of criticism."[12] If they were not written by a colored man, they would not sell enough to pay for the printing. I read them merely for facts, but I could appreciate the facts better if they were well presented. The book reminds me of a gentleman ~~clothed~~ in ~~rags~~ a dirty shirt. You are rather apt to doubt his gentility under such circumstances. I am sometimes doubtful of the facts for the same reason—they make but a shabby appearance. I am reading Molière's "Le Mari Confondu" or "the Cuckold". It is amusing.

---

11. In the margin a penciled note in a later hand adds: "(The expression is a proverb? from the latin?)"

12. *The Negro in the American Rebellion; His Heroism and His Fidelity*, by William Wells Brown, author of the *Narrative of William W. Brown, a Fugitive Slave* and the novel *Clotel*, was published in 1867 and republished in 1880. In *Notes on the State of Virginia* (1787) Thomas Jefferson had said of the African-born poet Phillis Wheatley, author of *Poems on Various Subjects, Religious and Moral:* "Never yet could I find that a Black had uttered a thought above the level of plain narration; never see even an elementary trait of painting or sculpture. . . . Religion indeed has produced a Phyllis Whately [*sic*]; but it could not produce a poet. . . . The compositions published under her name are below the dignity of criticism. The heroes of the Dunciad are to her, as Hercules to the author of that poem."

I had a rough time in school today. I had to keep my men in and lecture them about "wenching", as the Spectator hath it. Then the girls got to fighting this afternoon. The young folks seem to have "spring fever." I suppose the weather affects them somewhat like other animals. I am afraid they are told very little at home about correct principles. Oh, how they lie! It is shocking, but what can I do about it?

Sunday afternoon, April 10 / 81. Our Second Term Examination was over yesterday. I am quite fagged out. Examinations are very useful and necessary, but they are also very tiresome.

On Thursday, the Rev. C. A. Harvey, D.D.[,][13] Financial and Educational Sec'y of Howard University visited our school. He is on a tour of observation through the South, and is trying to do something in the interests of his school. I made him heartily welcome, and asked him to speak. He addressed the school a few minutes, and I was so well pleased that I invited him to speak at night. I had handbills printed and circulated and a right good house met at the Schoolhouse the same night. Dr. H. spoke very well, but at a disadvantage, he being not very well. He is very pleasant in conversation, betrays no trace of prejudice, invited me to visit him or write to him at Washington at any time. Louis spoke to him after the meeting, and he offered him fine inducements to attend Howard. Louis has since decided, I understand, to go next year.[14] I sincerely hope he will. It will be the making of him.

May 4, 1881.—Wednesday Night. Well! my time is so fully occupied with necessary business, that it is seldom I think to give a few minutes to my Journal. But I must not neglect it altogether.

Several things have happened lately which lead me to think that the colored man [is] moving upward very fast. The Prohibition movement has the effect of partly breaking down the color line, and will bring the white and colored people nearer together, to their mutual benefit. Some of the white teachers in

13. The Reverend Charles A. Harvey served as financial and educational secretary at Howard from 1878 to 1887.
14. Howard University has no record of Lewis Chesnutt's having enrolled as a student.

the Graded School came down to visit our school a few weeks ago, and one of them gave us quite a puff in the "Examiner." I am evidently in the good graces of the best people of the State.

The "Colored Presbytery of Yadkin" have been in session here for nearly a week. I invited them down to visit our school, and yesterday they made a *"reconnaissance* in force", and seemed to be very well pleased. We made a requisition on them for "gas," which they supplied in considerable quantity; their advice was excellent. A more intelligent body of colored men have never met in our town before.

I have received a sample copy of "Rumor[,]"[15] a New York paper, of which Walter Sampson is one of the editors. It echoes the popular clamor against the Garfield Administration for its scanty recognition of the claims of the colored office-seekers. *Tempora mutantur!* If the Democrats adopt an equally fair ~~programme~~ platform, and bid higher for our support, why shouldn't they get it? I'm a Republican on principle, but if the nigger is one-fourth of the party he ought to have one-tenth of the offices. Jno. Leary has one—Deputy Collector, *vice* Downing–removed.[16]

Thursday, July 21. It is really disheartening sometimes to turn back a few pages in one's journal, and read the plans projected for work or study, and then to think how poorly they have been

15. The *Rumor,* which began publication in New York in 1880, identified itself as "A Representative Colored American Paper." George Parker is listed as its publisher. *Tempora mutantur:* "times change."

16. Black support for the Republican party became somewhat unsettled after 1876, when Republican administrations began to court Democrats' votes in the reenfranchised South. Though some blacks were appointed to major federal offices at this time—Frederick Douglass was named recorder of deeds in the District of Columbia, and P. B. S. Pinchback was made surveyor of the port of New Orleans—most black patronage appointments in the Garfield and Arthur administrations were to menial positions, and the issue of federal appointments was a major subject of black political complaint. Chesnutt's views here echo those of the Colored State Convention held in Raleigh in June 1881 and of major black newspapers; for instance, the *New York Age* and the *Washington Bee.*

The last line of the entry is obscure. John Leary is probably John S. Leary, a noted black lawyer of Fayetteville, but I have been unable to confirm his appointment as deputy collector. George Thomas Downing (1819–1913) of Rhode Island was a prominent black civil rights activist who broke with the Republican party in the early 1880s.

followed, how little has been done. But such is poor human nature. If all the men who have a high ideal could reach it, the world would be full of scholars and saints. I have the greatest desire to become good—to become a *man* in the highest sense of the word. I recognize the fact that my profession requires it of me; but with all my efforts I can only partially, very imperfectly succeed.

Sometimes when I think of my shortcomings, I feel inclined to lay the blame to the circumstances with which I am surrounded. But a little reflection soon shows me that there is no condition in life, in which one is not frequently exposed to temptations. There is no merit in being good where there is no inducement to do evil. The discipline, the strength of character, the mastery of the will which come from resisting the evil—these are what make the man.

I have just finished "Wickersham's School Economy,["] [17] and its perusal suggested the above train of thought. I believe that, except the living example of a pure life, there is no agency so potent for leading the youthful mind to high aspirations as good books. Happy is the man who can read and appreciate the history, real or ideal, of a good man's life; and happier still is he who possesses the firmness and perseverence to carry out the good resolutions which the reading of such books always leads him to form. The writer of such a book as "David Copperfield" or "John Halifax" gives to literature a moral force, whose effect upon the young of future generations is simply incalculable.

I ought to be a good man—a far better one than I am. Providence has smiled upon me hitherto. At an age when most men are in school, I find myself at the head of a State institution, at a salary which many an A.M. of a good Northern College would be glad to get; a growing reputation; the respect and confidence of the best people in the community; a faithful and affectionate wife; two lovely and interesting children; a long and brilliant career of usefulness probably before me. What can hinder my succeeding in the effort to be all that a man and an educator should be? In any light I may look at it, the advantages of my

17. *School Economy: A Treatise on the Preparation, Organization, Employments, Government, and Authorities of Schools* (1864), by James Pyle Wickersham, state superintendent of public instruction in Pennsylvania and former principal of the Pennsylvania State Normal School.

position outweigh the disadvantages, and the preponderance of good over evil is very, very great. If I fail in life, I shall be content to acknowledge that the failure was my own fault. *Peccavi!* [18] my punishment is just.

But I will succeed. I will fight the opposing forces. I will learn to control myself. I will keep my mind's eye fixed constantly upon that high ideal, and strive to attain it. The saying is trite, but not the less true, "Where there's a will, there's a way."

I am reading a course of professional literature at present. *Root's School Amusements,* [19] and Wickersham's *School Economy* I have already completed, and derived valuable information from both. I expect to devote the remainder [of] that part of the vacation which I spend in Fayetteville to preparation for the next session. When I leave for Carthage [20] I shall take a Latin method, a Greek grammar, Shakespeare, and a few other books. In three months I can store away a vast amount of mental pabulum, which will provision my mind for future voyages. I thought I would devote the summer to writing, but there is so much that I do not know and ought, that I shall hardly write more than an occasional letter to a newspaper, and a few lectures for the next school year.

I have found an old picture of Susie taken several years before she was married. She was not pretty, but she was *good*—the picture shows it. I was lucky in my marriage. If I were on the carpet now, I should not know which way to turn for a woman I could admire and *respect.* They do not seem to understand the first principles of maidenly modesty or even common self-respect. I shall try to raise my daughters on a different plan.

I think I shall begin on Ethel's education next fall. I would like to test the kindergarten, and I think I could experiment very well with her. She is intelligent enough to begin it I presume.

Thursday, Aug 4, 81. Election day.   The question of Prohibition or free whiskey will be decided to-day. We had a large and en-

18. "I have sinned."

19. *School Amusements; or, How to Make School Interesting. Embracing Simple Rules for Military and Gymnastic Exercises, and Hints upon the General Management of the School Room,* by N. W. Taylor Root. This book was published in 1857 and had been reissued in 1876.

20. Carthage is the county seat of Moore County, west of Fayetteville, where Susan Chesnutt and the children spent the summer months.

thusiastic Prohibition meeting at the Market House last night. The antis had their row at Liberty Point. I made a rather poor speech; Scurlock and Slocumb very good ones. Our campaign has brought out a number of quiet men to the front.

Tomorrow I go up to Carthage with Elder Grange to see my wife and babies. They have been away for about a month, and my father-heart yearns for them. I will take Shakespeare and a Mental Philosophy, a Logic, and a few other books to amuse myself with. From Susie's account, the weather is much pleasanter there than here.

Dec 31st '81. This is the last night of the old year—a fit time to take retrospect of the old, and to make good resolutions for the new. But I am too lazy to-night to do either the one or the other. So I shall close my journal, and read King Henry the Sixth. I read Henry the Fifth the other night. Falstaff was a jolly old rogue, ancient Pistol a cowardly braggart, Fluellen an amusing character. I saw the play acted by Rignold[21] some years ago, and in it the part of Fluellen and his "disciplines of the Roman wars" was very well rendered indeed. Good-by old year! Welcome, new! [a]nd as the poet would probably remark, "Do well by me, and I'll the same by you."

Jan 16—82. Autograph written a few days ago for J. B. Small.

> Weary worker, faint not thou,
> Nor beneath thy burden bow:
> God will give to thee rich treasure,
> Rest, and peace, and endless pleasure,
> In a land above.

January 16, 1882

1.

> Every moment is a penny,
> In the currency of time,

21. George Rignold, who had been a "leading man" at the Theater Royal at Manchester, England, came to the United States to play the lead in Charles Calvert's production of *Henry V*, which was imported from Manchester, scenery and all, for the 1874–75 season. After 1875 Rignold's career went downhill and he took to the country, playing *Henry V* and other roles in many provincial cities.

Every ~~hour~~ fleeting hour a nickel,
Every day a dime.

2.

All your life's a precious fortune,
It is yours to spend or keep,
                    waste
Waste it not in sinful folly,
Indolence or sleep.

3.

Spend your time in work and study,
They are banks that will not break,
And the shining bonds they issue,
        None refuse to take.

4.

        pay
They will give a generous interest
And they never water stock;
In every mart ~~everywhere~~ you'll find their credit
        Solid as a rock.

5.

Then take care of every dollar,
Every nickel, every dime,
Every penny in the precious
        Currency of time!

Saturday

Feb 18, 1882. Last night I paid Mr. Hodges,[22] my tutor, ten dollars, balance due for two months instruction in Greek. He is a very nice young man, a thorough Southerner, but also a gentleman. My intercourse with him was pleasant enough; he is a college graduate—Davidson College, and pretty well informed, but without much taste for literature, as I have scarcely seen a book in his room for four months except his medical books, which I suppose he has been studying diligently.

I have now spent four months in the study of Greek, and

22. James Allison Hodges graduated from Davidson College in 1879, became a doctor in Fayetteville, and went on to a distinguished career. Vice president of the North Carolina Medical Society in the mid-1890s, he later joined the faculty of the University College of Medicine in Richmond and became president of the Virginia Medical Society. Hodges died in 1936.

according to my plans for the session, I must now stop, and devote my time to phonography and composition, in preparation for a different work from the one I am now engaged in. I hope to write two hundred words a minute in two months time. My friend Hodges has paid me some high compliments; as he is a Southerner, I suppose I ought to feel highly gratified,

"Praise from Sir Hubert Stanly is praise indeed"[23]

but, I have become so accustomed to it, and to the narrow prejudice which prevents it from bringing any substantial rewards, that I am afraid I don't appreciate it as I ought.

How Bro. Douglas Perry was Called To Preach.

Dug had been to meeting, and taken part. As he went home, all alone. He heard a bull frog calling distinctly. "Bro. Dug, go preach the Gospel"; "Bro Dug, etc." It weighed on his mind etc.

Judge B.—is so absentminded that he went home one rainy night and, putting his umbrella carefully to bed[,] went and stood himself up by the door to drip. Miss Beck soon set him straight, however.[24]

Lines

Written in Lady's (Miss L. Leary's) Album, Feb, 1882.

What shall I wish thee, lady fair,
Pleasure, or gold, or jewels rare,
Or a lover true thy life to share?
May they all be thine, my lady fair!

March 7. 82. "What is your name?" "J. M. Lloyd." "What is the J. for?" "Jere." "And the M.[?]" "Miah, sah; J for Jere and M for Miah."

I am reading a memoir of Sydney Smith.[25] It is interesting, but not so much so as Macaulay's Life and Letters. What a blessing is literature, and how grateful we should be to the publishers who

---

23. A once-famous quotation from Thomas Morton's 1797 play *A Cure for the Heartache.*
24. A marginal comment reads: "I thought this was new. It is as old as the hills."
25. Famous for having asked who in the four corners of the globe reads an American book, Sydney Smith (1771–1845) was an Edinburgh clergyman and wit. *A Memoir of the Rev. Sydney Smith* was published by his daughter Lady Holland in 1855.

have placed its treasures within reach of the poorest. Twenty cents for a book which in England would cost at least a pound! Shut up in my study, without the companionship of one congenial mind, I can enjoy the society of the greatest wits and scholars of England, can revel in the genius of her poets and statesmen, and by a slight effort of the imagination, find myself in the company of the greatest men of earth. Can work procure success? My only fear is that I will spoil it all by working too much.

I hear colored men speak of their "white friends". I have no white friends. I could not degrade the sacred name of "Friendship" by associating it with any man who feels himself too good to sit at table with me, or to sleep at the same hotel. True friendship can only exist between men who have something in common, between equals in something, if not in everything; and where there is respect as well as admiration. I hope yet to have a friend. If not in this world, then in some distant future eon, when men are emancipated from the grossness of the flesh, and mind can seek out mind; then shall I find some kindred spirit, who will sympathize with all that is purest and best in mine, and we will cement a friendship that shall endure throughout the ages.

I get more and more tired of the South. I pine for civilization, and "equality." I sometimes hesitate about deciding to go, because I am engaged in a good work, and have been doing, I fondly hope, some little good. But many reasons urge me the other way; and I think I could serve my race better in some more congenial occupation. And I shudder to think of exposing my children to the social and intellectual proscription to which I have been a victim. Is not my duty to them paramount? And can I not find hundreds who will do gladly, and as well, the work which I am doing?

Feb.—1882.

> A rosy glow came up in the east,
> Like the first ~~faint~~ vivid blush of a maiden's love,
> And, pale with the hate of a mistress discarded,
> The moon grew white in the heaven above.
> I rose from my couch in haste and cried,

"O sun, I welcome thy healing beams;
They bring me from night, and from seeming and shadows,
To the land of the real, where nothing seems;
        (and)
Where life, with all its realities grand,
Its joys and its treasures are at my command,
Then welcome, sun! with thee the day,
In happiness shall pass away."

The dying sun sank low in the west,
Bathing the sky with a crimson flood,
As the robe of a warrior, done to death
Is stained with the tide of his ebbing blood.
Then I folded my tired hands and cried,
"Welcome, night! thy moon's cold ray,
Shall woo me to slumber and take me away,
Out of the hurry and heat of the day,
     (lead)
And carry me into the land of dreams,
Where nothing is real, but only seems;
Where life, and all its realities sad,
Its so little of good and its much of bad,
        (away)
~~Are~~ is vanished and gone, and in my dreams,
Though all is seeming yet good it seems.

February, 1882.—

(1)

My little son in his cradle lay,
Softly rocked by his mother's hand;
Idly musing at close of day,
Came in my mind these fancies grand:—

(2)

My little boy, with his eyes of blue,
Though he was but of humble birth,
Yet should be wise, and brave, and true,
Yet should stand with the great of earth.

(3)

I saw him grow into a gallant youth,

Tender and hopeful, and brave and true,
       knowledge
Seeking in learning   to find the truth,
Eager   to think and eager to do.
(Ready)

(4)

I saw him standing in lofty halls,
Lifting his voice in the cause of right,
He opens his lips and from them falls,
A stream of eloquence, warm and bright.

I saw him holding the helm of state,
Called by a nation to be its head;
Plenty and peace on his ministry wait,
Wrongs were righted, the hungry fed.—

My little boy sickened, alas! and died,
And I wept for his dimpled face;
He was my darling, my hope, my pride;
He was all beauty and love and grace.

And not alone for my babe I wept,
With his dimpled face and eyes of blue:
Mourned I too for the gallant youth,
Who was so hopeful, and tender and true.

I mourned for the statesman wise and strong;
Never with eloquent tongue or pen,
Fearlessly should he oppose the wrong,
Fearlessly strive for the right of men.

I wept for the loss of a nation's chief,
He who would govern so long and well,
I bore the load of a nation's grief,
Grief that my pen can never tell.

And yet it was only my boy that died;
He cannot be great where mortals dwell,
But what he may be in another sphere,
Only an angel's voice could tell.

This poem is defective, and still needs revision. I copy it for preservation, so that I may have it at hand for future *limae labor.*[26] Two stanzas that come together, have the same rhymes. *True + blue, true and do.* Eager to do is all right, but I think *eager to think* can be improved upon. There are several weak verses—ballast, or wadding, but I must eliminate them; and the last verse hardly suits the argument of the poem, which is to show that fancy lent poignancy to my grief.

A Perplexed Nigger

Feb. 1882.

I'm "quite an intelligent nigger",
    words
As *the phrase* in our section go,
And I live in the land where the rice,
And the corn and the cotton grow.
I'm quite an ambitious nigger,
But the Democrats now being in,
I'm afraid I can't get elected
To the Legislature again.

2.

As I have no remarkable fondness,
For handling the plow or the hoe,
Boot-blacking or driving a carriage,
Which I had to do not long ago;
And having no great predilection,
For living on bacon and greens,
I'll adopt a respectable calling,
And write for the magazines.

3.

I know that the country is somewhat
Inclined to be down on the nigger,
For W—tt-k-r at West Point and F——r[27]

26. "labor of revision or polishing."
27. F——r here and in stanza 5 is Henry Ossian Flipper, the sixth black appointed to the U.S. Military Academy but the first to graduate. W—t-k-r is Johnson Chestnut Whittaker, onetime member of the West Point Class of 1880. Both were the subjects of particularly nasty histories, to which Chesnutt alludes in this poem.
    The Florida-born Henry O. Flipper endured an almost continual silent treatment during his years at West Point. After his graduation in 1877 Flipper was

I confess have cut quite a poor figure[.]
The one seems rather a coward,
The other—well even a *good* school
    an't
Couldn't make a brave man of a coward
Or make a wise man of a fool.

4.

And it's right good American logic,
Indeed it's the general belief,
When a nigger can't prove himself honest,
He certainly must be a thief.
A white man's regarded as honest,
Until his rascality's shown,
But a nigger, you know, is different
As "we white folks" have always known.

---

stationed at various forts in Indian Territory. In 1881, while stationed at Fort Davis, he was charged with embezzling government funds. Although found not guilty of this charge at his subsequent court martial, he was convicted of "conduct unbecoming an officer and a gentleman" and dismissed from the service of the United States. Flipper later speculated that the fact that he had gone riding with a young white woman lay behind the charges against him. A principal exhibit of the careers open to black talent and their vicissitudes in the early 1880s, Flipper's case would have been known to Chesnutt from his 1878 memoir *The Colored Cadet at West Point* and from intense media coverage.

Johnson C. Whittaker, from South Carolina, was admitted to the Military Academy in 1876. Less quiescent than Flipper to the racist conduct they both endured, Whittaker had a correspondingly harder time in his West Point years. When a white cadet struck him in a quarrel Whittaker avoided fighting back, conduct which had caused an earlier black cadet to be officially condemned, and instead reported him; but this course won him the reputation of a coward. On April 6, 1880, he was found unconscious in his room, his feet tied to his bedstead, his hands bound together, his hands and feet mutilated, his hair hacked, and his earlobes slashed. Judging it inconceivable that white cadets could have performed this act, the commandant, General Schofield, decided that Whittaker had faked the incident and that his injuries were self-inflicted. A subsequent court of inquiry found against Whittaker, and after another lengthy inquiry Whittaker was officially found guilty of self-mutilation, dishonorably discharged, and sentenced to one year of hard labor. Later in the year of Chesnutt's poem President Chester A. Arthur overturned this sentence on the grounds of improper admission of evidence. Whittaker was reinstated to the Military Academy but almost immediately redischarged for deficiency in Natural Philosophy. He lived until 1931.

5.[28]

And since W——r cut his own ears,
Or at least cant prove the contrary[,]
That all niggers would do just the same,
Is a very safe corollary.
Since F——r's accused of stealing,
Or was careless in keeping accounts,
Any nigger will steal and be careless
—That's exactly to what it amounts.

6.

Down here, if a crime is committed,
And the criminal cannot be found,
Suspicion will rest on a nigger,
If there's one in a mile around.
And ~~then if~~ when the ~~nigger's~~ accused is imprisoned,
If guilty they don't wait to see;
They take him away from the jailer
And swing him right up to a tree.

7.

A white man is tried by a jury,
And with plenty of friends and red tape,
And the best friend of all—ready money—
Has at least a fair chance to escape.
But a nigger, perforce, must be guilty,
Because—any nigger in fact,
Under similar circumstances,
Would be capable of the act.

8.

And it matters not whether he's guilty
Or not, it is nothing but right,
If he's likely to do any mischief,
To hang him for fear that he might.
And when white folks see anything clearly
In this particular light,
They don't hesitate for a moment,
To do what they think to be right.

---

28. In the journal this stanza is lightly crossed out.

9.

I'm quite an intelligent nigger,
But such things I cannot understand,
When all men are free and equal,
By the highest law of the land.
I'm quite an intelligent nigger,
But I cannot exactly see,
Why there's one set of laws for the white folks,
And a different set for me.

10.

Perhaps some wise white man or other
The riddle will kindly explain,
Why justice and Christian charity
Are different for different men.
Why they set us aside in the churches
And in the common schools,
And in the insane asylums
They separate even the fools[.]

11.

And some intellects philosophic,
Have thought that even in Heaven,
A sort of kitchen department
To colored folks will be given.
There's but one place ~~they don't separate us~~
   we're not separated,
The reason I'm sure I can't tell,
But no one has yet thought proper,
To separate us in Hell!
   (set us aside)

"Jess' so the tree fall, jes' so it lie,
Jes' so the sinner live, jes' so he die".
                              Rev. David Williams.

Character—the inquisitive nuisance.

Sept. 8.[29]

I will dry my tears, for I have no fear
But that death was to him the birth,
Into a higher and broader sphere,
Than the longest lease of life on earth.

And the honors the humblest angel bears
(Heaven)
Shine in that land with a brighter glow,
Than all the gems a monarch wears,
In the crown of the greatest realm below.

Write up story of the effect produced by a deadly telegram falling in the midst of a peaceful household, and scattering confusion before it was opened.[30] Parties concerned were Will Henderson[']s parents. Burst into tears, and alarmed the neighborhood. Certain that Sary Ann was dead, and they was a' goin' to bring her home. On being asked what was in the telegram, didn't know. On being opened it was from Ben saying that he would arrive on the 10 o'clock train.

Elder Small and his African wife. Mysterious affair. Elder Small and his first wife. Old planter or store-keeper. Daughter named Rose. Order-Room clerk. How the correspond. was conducted through the old cake-woman. First friend to whom Mr. S. revealed the proposed marriage told a lady friend; second told his wife. License obtained, as it would not do to put up banns. Met her opposite police station. Just then up comes old man a[nd] carries Rose off. She goes home, feigns toothache, takes off Sunday clothes, puts on old bonnet, takes of[f] jewelry and all. She sets friend to watch on one street, he on another. Meet marry church filled as if by magic. Meet old woman on my way home[.] Slap, hug, kiss. "O Rose, how could you deceive us so! If you were going to marry the man why didn't you say so." Went on to new house. New dresses. Old man wouldn't speak. Ran back one day, "Mother in law says I ought to speak." Met again. No speak. Finally find old man at somebody else's

29. Chesnutt here inserts: "See p. 41" (the journal page that contains the end of his "defective" poem on the death of a son).
30. A marginal comment reads: "Old."

house Rose in lap. Wouldn't speak. Takes him home, best port wine from officer's mess. "When I want to see you I will come but don't darken my doors." "Walk a piece of the way with me Rose" "A little further." "Finally go in old man's house." Grand Reconciliation. Tableau. After that nothing like my son in law.

Mary McNeill and Sarah. Abortive attempt to spirit Mary away to Wilmington[.] Frustrated by a note from Sarah to Cap'n forbidding him to take her. Bound to McNeill.

Lucy Pearce. Romantic story—foundling. Raised by Mrs. Halliday.

Slaves stealing bacon—called it "light-wood" when sold to peddlars.

Character—Leading Colored Man. Went about immediately after the war organizing secret Societies. First organize society —fee one dollar— 3 months later, 1st Degree, 50¢. 3 mo. later 2nd degree. 50¢ etc. Next yr. Another society. Union League. Good Temp. Gd Samaritan, Masons, etc.

Colored People eat rat in the rice district of S.C. Elder ate largely of squirrels at supper. Heard little boy say "Mamma I 'ant some more rat." Horrified. Next day "Elder you don't seem for to like rats much." Wouldn't do to say so hurt your feelings.

Preacher
(Fellow) wanted woman. Told he[r] to go under tree and pray to the Lord asking if it were right. He climbed the tree and answered.

Half-witted fellow, about to be baptized:
Fellow says "Hold on, I'll be ——— if you baptize me in anybody's name but my own."

Panorama Experiences.
Wanted to give ex in church. All trustees willing but one, long lank fellow black. He got up and said Look heah Mr. you [the rest of the page is in shorthand.]

Baggage man refused to check box. It was night. L. went to conductor, who in the darkness or by the dim light took him for drummer. "Conductor, this is an outrage; I can't get my baggage checked or put on train.["] "John put this gent's baggage on the train. It's all right sir, against rules to check anything but trunks.["] Next morning conductor saw shabby clothes by day-light. "John, put that young man's box off."

———————

~~Brudders &~~ "Bretherings & Sisterings De Chesnutt Bro is gwine to gib a pamberam here tomorrow night" Pres. E[l]der over his shoulder "a *Panorama*" Bros. Sis. "I made a mistake it is a pamaramadam."   Bob da's gwine be a new thing at the church tonight, "What is it Jim anyhow? Its a fantastic— somethin', and I'll see it if I have to crawl to get there.

John Green's list of 43 different remedies for rheumatism.[31] One was carry a Buck-eye—, another, cut a slit in your leg and put a pea in it—let it stay till it sprouts.

"Incorrect, sir: them boys over there's talking." "How could you look at your lesson Johnnie, and at the same time see those boys talking?" "I—I—I didn't see 'em talking sir: I—I smelt 'em."

31. Chesnutt again alludes to John Green's *Recollections of the Inhabitants, Localities, Superstitions, and Kuklux Outrages of the Carolinas,* which takes a dim view of folk customs and beliefs.

INDEX

Abbott, Lyman, 96–97
Alston, Rev. William J., 43, 45
Atkins, Joseph, 49

Barnes, A. S., 48; Barnes's *History of the United States,* 47–48, 50
Blaine, James G., 114
Blair, Hugh, 17; *Lectures on Rhetoric and Belles Lettres,* 93–99
Boyd [Hardinge], Belle, 67
Bradley, Nellie H., *The First Glass,* 54–56
Brown, William Wells, *The Negro in the American Rebellion,* 164
Bruce, Blanche Kelso, 115
Brumidi, Constantino, 114
Bryan, R. K., 140
Bryant and Stratton's Common School Bookkeeping, 80
Bunyan, John, 121
Burns, Robert, 44, 75, 77, 121; "Auld Lang Syne," 75–76; "Eppie Adair," 69; "To a Louse," 66, 109
Buxton, Joseph Potts, 46, 153
Buxton, Rebecca Bledsoe, 153
Byron, George Gordon, Lord, *Don Juan,* 12, 44, 71–72

Chesnutt, Andrew (father), 6, 76–78, 118, 136

Chesnutt, Ann (sister), 28
Chesnutt, Charles Waddell: and black professional class formation, 12–16; education of, 5–18; literary compositions, 46–47, 50–54, 63–66, 98–103, 119–21, 124, 150–52, 161–62, 169–79; literary plans and ambitions, 19–25, 121–22, 124–26, 139–40, 145–46, 154–56, 179–81; loneliness of, 25–26, 157–58, 172; political activities of, 46, 135–36, 160, 166; professional aspirations, 19–20, 74, 81, 106, 110–11, 118–19, 167–68; reading of, see listings of individual authors; and religion, 67, 69–70, 72–73, 77, 122–23, 129–32; teaching in rural schools, 9–12, 41–43, 59–62, 70–72, 74, 78–81; and vernacular culture, 12, 14, 22–25, 81–82, 112–13, 121–22, 129–32; visit to Washington, D.C., 108–19. *Works: The House Behind the Cedars,* 39; *The Marrow of Tradition,* 16; "The Perplexed Nigger," 175–78; "Tom's Warm Welcome," 155–56
Chesnutt, Dallas (uncle), 117–18
Chesnutt, Ethel (daughter), 105, 168
Chesnutt, Lewis (brother), 67, 75, 77–78, 111, 118, 143–44, 165

Chesnutt, Lillian (sister), 45

Chesnutt, Susan Perry (wife), 111, 117, 136, 168

Christian Union, 20, 96–97, 105, 106–108

Cicero, 90, 163

Cobb, Rev. S. B., 140–42

Cotten, Wesley, 159

Cowper, William, 12, 70, 75; *The Task,* 71–72

Craik, Dinah Maria Mulock, *John Halifax, Gentleman,* 104, 167

Crawford, Rev., 147–48

Davis, Elder J. W., 24, 122–23, 128–33, 158–59

Dickens, Charles, *Barnaby Rudge,* 50, 80; *David Copperfield,* 167

Downing, George Thomas, 166

Du Bois, W. E. B., 9, 15

Dumas, Alexandre (père), *The Count of Monte Cristo,* 92

Dwight, Mary Ann, *Grecian and Roman Mythology,* 88

East Lynne, or the Earl's Daughter, 56

Educator, The, 116

Fisk Jubilee Singers, 24, 106, 121

Flipper, Henry Ossian, 26, 175–77

Franklin, Benjamin, 2, 106

Freedman's Bureau, 5–6

Goethe, Johann Wolfgang von, 104; *Faust,* 149–50, 164

Goldsmith, Oliver, *Roman History,* 159

Graham, Alexander, 8, 148

Greeley, Horace, 106; *The American Conflict,* 163

Green, John Patterson, 149, 181

Haigh, George H., 126–28, 134, 152–53

Haigh, Dr. T. D., 3, 27, 105–106, 142

Harris, Cicero Richardson, 8–9, 39,
43, 48, 50, 54, 73, 76, 82–83

Harris, Robert, 5, 8, 14, 16–17, 22, 43, 45–46, 47, 48, 50, 85, 123, 134–35, 142, 143–44

Harvey, Rev. Charles A., 165

Hicks, Alexander, 162–63

Hill, Robert, 169–71

Hodges, James Allison, 170–71

Homer, *The Iliad,* 87–88

Howard, General O. O., 5

Howard School (Fayetteville), 5–9, 16–17, 22

Howard University, 116, 165

Hurston, Zora Neale, 24

Hyman, John A., 46

Jarvis, Thomas Jordan, 158

Jefferson, Thomas, 164

Kyle, William E., 3, 142

Ladd, John J., 104–105

Leary, John S., 28, 46, 166

Longfellow, Henry Wadsworth, "Hiawatha," 92

Macaulay, Thomas Babington, 89; *Life and Letters,* 159–60, 171

McLaughlin, John, 4, 160–61

Mann, Horace, 7

Mayhew, Ira, *The Means and Ends of Universal Education,* 79–82

Merivale, Charles, *General History of Rome,* 159, 163

Merrimon, Augustus S., 44–45

Molière, *Le Mari confondu,* 164

Moore, E. F., 147–48

Moore, Elder, 54

Neufeld, Emil, 141–43, 146–48

Niles, John Milton, *A View of South America and Mexico,* 50

Page, David Perkins, *Theory and Practice of Teaching,* 46, 50

Peabody Educational Fund, 5, 7–9

Peabody School (Charlotte), 8, 10
Peck, William Guy, *Elements of Mechanics*, 80
Pickens, William, 6, 9, 28
Powers, E. P., 135–36

Quackenbos, George Payne, *Advanced Course of Composition and Rhetoric*, 50, 158
Quintillian, 93

Ransom, Matt Whittaker, 115
Revels, Jonathan, 49
Richardson, George, 115
Richardson, Victoria, 48, 54, 58, 73, 76, 77
Rignold, George, 169
Root, N. W. Taylor, *School Amusements*, 168
Rumor, The, 166
Russell, Daniel Lindsay, 115, 128–29, 133

Sampson, Walter, 166
Sankey, Ira, *Gospel Hymns*, 122
Scurlock, George, 148–49, 169
Shadd, Furmann J., 116
Shakespeare, William, 163, 168–69; *Measure for Measure*, 44; *Henry V*, 169; *Henry VI*, 169
Slave Songs of the United States, 24, 121
Slocumb, Albert H., 147, 169
Smith, Sydney, 171
Star of Zion, 161
State Colored Normal School (Fay-

etteville), 8, 14, 16–17, 25, 26, 85, 107, 158, 162–63, 165–66
Stephens, Alexander Hamilton, 114–15
Stowe, Harriet Beecher, *Uncle Tom's Cabin*, 50, 125

Tennyson, Alfred, Lord, 164
Thackeray, William Makepeace, *Vanity Fair*, 154
Todd, Rev. John, *Student's Manual*, 88–89
Tourgée, Albion, 21–22; *A Fool's Errand*, 21, 124–25, 149

Union League, 161

Vance, Zebulon Baird, 114–15
Virgil, 105, 148; *The Aeneid*, 90–92
Voltaire, 89–92

Walton, Izaac, 139
Washington, Booker T., 6, 13, 27
Wells, Samuel Roberts, *A Handbook for Home Improvement*, 12, 14, 40–41
Wheatley, Phillis, 164
White, George H., 162–63
Whittaker, Johnson Chestnut, 26, 175–77
Wickersham, James Pyle, *School Economy*, 167–68
Williams, J. D., 135–36, 147
Woodworth, Samuel, "The Old Oaken Bucket," 81

Charles W. Chesnutt was an American novelist and essayist at the turn of the twentieth century. He wrote *The Conjure Woman, The House Behind the Cedars, The Marrow of Tradition, The Wife of His Youth and Other Stories,* and *The Colonel's Dream.*

Richard H. Brodhead is Housum Professor of English at Yale University and Dean of Yale College. He is author of *Hawthorne, Melville and the Novel, The School of Hawthorne,* and *Cultures of Letters: Scenes of Reading and Writing in Nineteenth Century America,* and has edited *The Conjure Woman and Other Conjure Tales* by Charles W. Chesnutt.

Library of Congress Cataloging-in-Publication Data
Chesnutt, Charles Waddell, 1858–1932.
The journals of Charles W. Chesnutt / edited by Richard H. Brodhead.
Includes bibliographical references and index.
ISBN 0-8223-1379-0 (cloth). — ISBN 0-8223-1424-X (pa)
1. Chesnutt, Charles Waddell, 1858–1932—Diaries. 2. Afro-American novelists—19th century—Diaries. I. Brodhead, Richard H., 1947– .
II. Title.
PS1292.C6Z47   1993
818.403—dc20
[B]   93-10872 CIP